THIS MEANS WAR

THIS MEANS WAR:

Equipping Christian Families for Fostercare or Adoption

By Cheryl Ellicott and Friends

Sweetwater Still

SPOKANE, WASHINGTON

ISBN: 978-0-9843599-4-3
LCCN: 2010924209

Published by
Sweetwater Still Publishing
Spokane, Washington

Printed in the United States of America

"There was a little girl, who had a little curl,
Right in the middle of her forehead.
When she was good, she was very good indeed,
But when she was bad she was horrid."
Henry Wadsworth Longfellow

About the Photographs:

When you choose to adopt, your decision affects everyone around you: your immediate family, relatives, friends, neighbors and even strangers who see you in the grocery store. Everyone's watching; everyone's talking. You're an inspiration to some or an oddity to others, but you impact them all.

Therefore, the photos in *This Means War* are not just our adopted children. They're here, but so are the biological children and even some friends and relatives. When you see their faces, suddenly adoption - even a difficult adoption - seems worth it. Suddenly, putting on the full armor of Christ, so you will continue to stand and protect the children, makes more sense.

Lastly, gossip hurts people; *This Means War* isn't meant to be a *tell-all*, therefore some names and identifying details have been changed.

CONTENTS

INTRODUCTION

This book is meant to educate, equip, and protect foster or adoptive families so they in turn can protect the homeless children of the world. The book is geared toward caretakers, parents and grandparents but I pray it'll also bring encouragement and understanding to those who were adopted.

If you're a family or individual hoping to do fostercare, adopt, or have recently adopted, chances are you weren't given enough information to prepare you for success. This book is a compilation of things I've learned and also stories shared with me by other parents.

Since 1989, I've worked with approximately 50 children. Together, Mike and I were house-parents to about 25 teens and pre-teens in crisis at a long-term shelter. We were foster parents to an additional 25 infants and toddlers in our home in subsequent years. We adopted three special needs children through the fostercare system and we have three biological children.

Mike spent over 15 years working with adults with disabilities and we did in-home care for that population as well. In 2001, I founded "Specialmom," a support group for foster and adoptive parents, which is still active today. Through this little family of like-minded parents, I've been encouraged as an adoptive mother and as a believer. I hope you also find a supportive group to hold you up in prayer and encourage you on this quest. In the meantime, I pray this book will prepare you to stand firmly and be used mightily for the Kingdom of God.

Without information and preparation, too many have waltzed in over their heads, fallen, and seen their families damaged. If the focus of this book seems negative, it should offset that you're probably wearing rose-colored glasses. You're most likely already envisioning the joy and success of loving an unloved child. You know it's more blessed to give than to receive. You believe God's version of love never fails. You expect you'll reap a harvest if you continue to do good and do not give up.

I want to prepare you for the fight to come in hopes that you'll persevere long enough to see that harvest.

> "You have persevered and have endured hardships for my name, and have not grown weary. Yet I hold this against you: You have forsaken your first love." (Rev 2:3-4)

If you learn only one thing from this book, let it be this: It's easy to get caught up in the work of a humanitarian and forget your main objective in life is to love God with all your heart, mind, body, and soul. The only way to succeed in life is to remain as a branch connected to the vine [Jesus]. Keep your relationship with God through Jesus as the most important thing -- the ONLY thing that matters -- and He will pour out His spirit on the children... in His time.

"Even youths grow tired and weary, and young men stumble and fall; but those who hope in the LORD will renew their strength. They will soar on wings like eagles; they will run and not grow weary, they will walk and not be faint." (Isaiah 40:30-31 NIV)

Part One:

The Parents

~❤~

1

First, the Bad News

Christian adoption is a declaration of war; you're challenging an enemy who is stronger and smarter than you.

First and foremost, if you're going to succeed in adoption, you must realize the significance of your actions in the spirit world. By adopting, your family is storming the gates of hell, and rescuing little, lost souls to bring them to safety and the light of the truth. Your only weapons are prayer, the power of the Holy Spirit, and the knowledge of God and His word. If this doesn't make sense to you, I ask that you go to the back of the book and work through the **Basics Bible Study** first.

If you've never thought much about "spiritual warfare," you're destined to learn the hard way. I'm not talking about the common myths and misconceptions called *spiritual warfare*, but the real thing as seen in the Bible – in the life of Jesus, the apostles, and other believers. Study the scriptures *as if your life depends upon knowing them!*

Pray and ask God to help you see the unseen battles you're in!

In fact, parents who've read *This Means War* suggest you *stop and pray right now*; ask God to help you make it past the diversions and *finish reading this book!*

Each time they picked this book up to read, they were distracted. Just like clockwork: the phone rang, there was a knock at the door, their spouse suddenly needed to talk, the dogs started barking, or the kids threw up. Some got suspicious and started reading the book *just to see what would go wrong next!* I'm not exaggerating. You should have seen my life while I was trying to write this book for you!

Satan doesn't fight fairly!

This is serious. You *need* the information in this book. Pray, and then read on regardless of distractions!

When you read the Gospel accounts in the Bible, you'll see that each time Jesus went in to a town or region, He did two things the same, regardless of where he was. Do you know what they were?

> One: He healed sick people.
> Two: He freed people from harassment, oppression,
> and possession by evil spirits.

Have you ever known anyone who was sick? That's a ridiculous question, but we must wake up and realize that harassment, oppression, and possession by evil spirits are just as common as physical sickness. If Satan went after *even Jesus*, he won't leave you alone. Once you see this, you'll be ready for the attacks you and your family are already experiencing.

In regard to adoption, understand that (usually) Satan has blinded and captured the biological parents of these "adoptable children" through lies and sin. He's already destroyed their families (and often they themselves) through sin. Now he intends to destroy their children. You're on the offensive. You want to enter Satan's territory and walk away with (what he views as) his property. Don't think he'll let you take them without a fight. You may be trying to adopt a child whose biological family has experienced centuries of darkness and possession.

Satan will attack you individually and as a family. Be prepared (put on the full armor of God) and you can stand; be caught off-guard and he'll damage your family, your witness, and your threat to his kingdom. The rest of this chapter will supply you with practical tips before we get into the issues and challenges typical with adoptable children.

Ready? Please take this seriously and beware of these things in your life!

These are some common ways he specifically attacks Moms:

He'll make you sick and tired to cripple you as a mother.

He'll try to isolate you from other godly women by keeping you away from church, Bible studies, and other times of fellowship.

He'll send worldly people to teach you lies; telling you they're the latest and greatest methods to help you raise children.

Be on your guard or you'll stop looking to Jesus; you'll focus on your ill health, the children's bad behavior, and an ever-increasing desire to learn new and improved methods of parenting. Instead of reading the Bible and seeking God, you'll look to people who have an ungodly world view for help and answers. Instead of spending time nurturing your relationship with your husband (this is the backbone of the family), your attention and energy will all go to the child or children.

These are some common ways Satan specifically attacks Dads:

He'll try to keep you away from your family so they're not protected, encouraged, or taught through you. This often comes in the guise of a "better job" offer, more hours at work, or a job that makes you so tired you're hardly awake, let alone praying fervently for your family.

He'll try to keep you away from church, Bible studies, and other times of fellowship with godly men; he wants you isolated so you're easier to defeat and so you're not encouraging others.

Satan will tempt you with a *me-centric* false version of Christianity. Instead of laying down your life, giving up your reputation and ambitions - living just to *know and love Jesus*, you'll do "Christian work" to feel good about yourself. Instead of denying yourself - humbly serving - you'll strive to know more than others so you can be their fearless leader.

He'll tempt you to let your guard down regarding morality: he'll say it's okay to expose yourself to questionable TV shows, movies, magazines, games, and conversations, etc.; it starts mild, and then progresses as you become dull and desensitized. He's waiting until you start allowing lust to rule your mind and then he'll send real temptations into your life, pushing for you to fall into sin. If you fall, you'll either confess (and the family will be damaged or destroyed) or you'll begin to hide the truth of your sin. If you're lying and hiding your sin, you'll be separated from God and his power, and your trust and relationship with your spouse will become diseased and may eventually die. While the above is going on, Satan will be whispering things to your spouse, telling both truths (about the things you're doing wrong) and lies, trying to drive a wedge between you.

Yes, these things happen to all believers, but the intensity increases when you involve yourself in ministry – the battle for souls. I can't stress how important this is to understand. In my many years as a believer, I've seen Satan step up his attack on every believer who decided to get involved in ministry! Many have very publicly fallen, others more privately. Again and again, families have been destroyed, ministries dissolved.

If you don't prepare yourself and guard against these things, you'll fall into a trap. Once you've fallen, unless you repent and confess your sins to God and *to the person you've wronged,* you'll remain trapped. The power of the Holy Spirit will leave you. You'll stop praying for your family, you'll become a poor example, or worse, and the children will no longer have a covering of spiritual protection.

Here's a note just for Dads: don't think that you're *supposed to be* the spiritual leader of the family. Realize this: whether you're falling or standing, you already *are* the spiritual leader.

Where you let yourself go, Satan will assume permission to take your children also.

> "In the paths of the wicked lie thorns and snares, but he who guards his soul stays far from them." (Proverbs 22:5 NIV)

Think that's bad? In case that wasn't enough, Satan will attack your family *through* the children:

Just as in the Vietnam War, American soldiers were unprepared when the enemy sent little children into their camps carrying grenades; Satan uses needy children to carry a bomb into the Christian family. The child is a victim, but so is the family, especially if they're unprepared to defend against the attack.

Some of the common baggage needy children come with are:

Fetal alcohol effects: Learning disabled, very little impulse control due to alcohol related brain damage.

Inability to bond: Extreme difficulty learning to return love or to consider others.

Sexually inappropriate behaviors: Some learned through exposure & abuse, some due to brain damage/lack of impulse control.

Learning disabilities: Sometimes temporary, but often permanent due to alcohol or drug exposure.

Violent tendencies: May have been learned, but often due to exposure to drugs inutero, neglect in infancy, emotional trauma, or inherited mental illness.

Mental Illness, bizarre or self-destructive behavior: Difficult to diagnose; many temporary emotional spiritual conditions mimic or produce these.

Extreme **manipulative skills:** Previously neglected or abused children often "divide and conquer" as a means of getting their way. They may purposely try to turn married couples against each other; many will use *false accusations* of abuse or molestation as a tool or means of revenge.

I pray that after reading this, you still want to adopt. As a Christian *on the offensive*, you're marked by the enemy. There's a price on your head (a bulls-eye on your forehead, if you will), and you cannot skip through life humming *"There's a Blue Bird on my Shoulder"* anymore. Yet I pray this information will not discourage you, but will make you more determined to fight for the lives of the helpless; this fight *can be won!*

How do we win the fight?

By *humbling ourselves* and submitting to God.

> "You adulterous people, don't you know that friendship with the world is hatred toward God? Anyone who chooses to be a friend of the world becomes an enemy of God. Or do you think Scripture says without reason that the spirit He caused to live in us envies intensely? But He gives us more grace. That is why Scripture says:

> "God opposes the proud but *gives grace to the humble.*"

Submit yourselves, then, to God. Resist the devil, and he will flee from you. Come near to God and He will come near to you. Wash your hands, you sinners, and purify your hearts, you double-minded. Grieve, mourn and wail. Change your laughter to mourning and your joy to gloom. *Humble yourselves before the Lord, and He will lift you up.*" (James 4:4-10 NIV)

"Put on the full armor of God so that you can take your stand against the devil's schemes. For our struggle is not against flesh and blood, but against the rulers, against the authorities, against the powers of this dark world and against the spiritual forces of evil in the heavenly realms. Therefore put on the full armor of God, so that when the day of evil comes, you may be able to stand your ground, and after you have done everything, to stand." (Ephesians 6:11-13 NIV)

2

Now, For the Good News

We are more than conquerors, when FIGHTING BACK in the spirit.

"Who shall separate us from the love of Christ? Shall trouble or hardship or persecution or famine or nakedness or danger or sword? As it is written:
'For your sake we face death all day long; we are considered as sheep to be slaughtered.' No, in all these things we are more than conquerors through him who loved us. For I am convinced that neither death nor life, neither angels nor demons, neither the present nor the future, nor any powers, neither height nor depth, nor anything else in all creation, will be able to separate us from the love of God that is in Christ Jesus our Lord." (Romans 8:35-39 NIV)

A good friend of ours wrote a song that I think really applies here. One line says this:

"Lord, You never left me, but I fell behind."

Nothing and no one can separate us from the love of God in Christ Jesus. But *can* we be separated from Jesus? Surely His love for us will always remain, but scripture is clear that, yes, we can be defeated. We can turn back, fall away, or "fall behind" when walking with the Lord. We must make a constant effort to stay in step with the Spirit.

> "Those who belong to Christ Jesus have crucified the sinful nature with its passions and desires. Since we live by the Spirit, let us keep in step with the Spirit." (Galatians 5:24-25 NIV)

Here are some practical things you can do to stand firmly and stay in step with the Spirit:

When you suddenly become sick or unexplainably tired, know that Satan sees you as a threat; he's trying to stop you.

Determine to fight back: Get up, work hard, smile, sing praises, pray for your family, and act like a nice parent even when you aren't feeling nice... *especially* when you aren't feeling nice!

Get suspicious. Why is Satan trying to slow you down and make you ineffective now? Suspect he's planning an attack on your children or other loved ones and doesn't want you awake, alert, and involved. Pray that God will fill you with His Holy Spirit; ask Him to protect your family. Ask God for the strength to drag yourself around on your family's behalf if that's what it takes.

When the illness tactic doesn't stop you, Satan often stops attacking there and moves on to something else.

Determine to guard your health and stay off mood or mind altering medicines whenever possible. Stay alert! Even prescription drugs often cause depression and worse side effects; they interfere with your ability to think clearly and make wise choices. They have the same effect on children, and special needs children may have intensified reactions to even over the counter medications. Ask God to heal you and show you how to use prevention to protect your health.

Satan will try to keep you away from church, Bible studies, and other times of fellowship with godly believers or any actions of ministry. He wants you isolated so you're easier to defeat and not encouraging others.

When you desire to let God live through you and use you to set people free from Satan's hold, the Holy Spirit will prompt you to get involved in a Bible teaching church and other fellowship groups or ministries.

You'll know you're following God's lead (and that Satan is trying to stop you) when something like this happens when you try to attend:

☹ You wake up with a headache and a bad case of hemorrhoids.

☹ You find that the cat has peed on your clean laundry. (Luckily, you find one last clean shirt in a bag leftover from a vacation.)

☹ The baby starts throwing up. (All over your clean shirt.)

☹ Your older children get into a fight over toothpaste; one gets a bloody nose, the other a black eye.

☹ Your beloved relative calls in a fit and needs you to solve all of the problems of your dysfunctional family, right now.

☹ The dog bites the cat.

☹ You go out to start the car and see that someone has broken out the back window.

☹ Your spouse gets angry and wants to sit down and talk about either divorcing or killing you.

Determine to resist Satan's tricks by *going to church (or Bible study, etc.) anyway!*

☺ Take a Tylenol and use some Preparation H.

☺ Clean up the baby, go next door (in your robe if need be) and borrow a shirt from your neighbor.

☺ Give the kid with the bloody nose some tissue and hand out a bag of ice for the other's eye.

☺ Tell your beloved relative that you'll be home and ready to talk in a few hours, but if things get too bad while you're gone they should call 911.

☺ Put the dog in his kennel and pray for the cat (as you pass him on your way out the door).

☺ Duct tape some plastic over the empty hole in the back of the car where the window used to be.

☺ Tell your spouse you'd be happy to talk about their desire to divorce or kill you. Set an appointment for this discussion *after* church is over.

Then hit the road and don't stop for anything. Laugh when your hair starts sticking up, your breath suddenly gets really stinky, you have gas, the driver in the car behind you honks for no reason (or maybe they don't like the duct tape), the driver in front of you flips you off, the kids drop the baby's diaper bag out the window and you get a flat tire. You're on a mission; pray that God will help you get there and don't let anything distract you.

Once you've made up your mind and pushed past the distractions a few times, you'll see how predictable they are and their intensity might decrease. The enemy will leave... and *look for a more opportune time.*

Are you suddenly having lustful, hateful, or otherwise sinful thoughts about someone?

I see these probable "fiery darts" as a warning bell or the sounds of a snarling guard dog; I've just come *too close* to someone whom Satan was attacking or guarding fiercely. Because the spirit of God lives in me, I'm a powerful threat. Satan wants to push me away from that person as far and fast as he can. I suspect he's flooding my mind, hoping I'll let it catch fire (and then be guilty) or that I'll just feel guilty and run away.

If this happens, ask God to forgive you for the thoughts in your head (maybe they came from your own sinful nature) and to clean your mind and heart. Then, go on the offensive! Fervently pray for the person that Jesus will set them free from Satan's grasp. Pray they'll be lifted out of the pit they're in. If unbelievers, pray their eyes will be opened to the Good News of Christ's redeeming work to save them. Anytime the thoughts return, pray for the person again; pray and ask God what He wants you to do. Put this person on a prayer list and if God opens a door, share the hope that's inside you, but never put yourself in a position that could be misinterpreted or lead to sin. One example: Don't spend time alone with someone of the opposite sex nor enter into a friendship of this type; even if it doesn't turn into something ugly, it looks bad and may be misinterpreted or used to hurt people. Refer them to a godly person of their own gender for friendship and counsel.

"Watch and pray so that you will not fall into temptation. The spirit is willing, but the body is weak." (Mark 14: 38 NIV)

"The weapons we fight with are not the weapons of the world. On the contrary, they have divine power to demolish strongholds. We demolish arguments and every pretension that sets itself up against the knowledge of God, and we take captive every thought to make it obedient to Christ." (2 Corinthians 10:4-5 NIV)

"In addition to all this, take up the shield of faith, with which you can extinguish all the flaming arrows of the evil one." (Ephesians 6:16 NIV)

Satan will try to separate you from your spouse and children (by too many hours at work, too many extracurricular activities, etc).

Know that Satan sees your family unit as a threat, so he's trying to separate you. Determine that you will fight back: Refuse to conform to how the world lives; bigger houses, shinier cars, and more extracurricular activities. Don't love money and become a slave to your job. Don't remain trapped in debt because you're greedy for more *stuff*. Don't waste valuable family time entranced by television, movies, computer games, and books. Protect your family from the influences of these things, which are usually *pretty packaging* on an ugly and ungodly, false message. Spend time alone with your family, getting to know them. Listen to your spouse and children and share your heart with them daily.

> "For the love of money is a root of all kinds of evil. Some people, eager for money, have wandered from the faith and pierced themselves with many griefs." (1 Timothy 6:10 NIV)

Satan will send people to teach you lies, telling you they're the latest and greatest methods by which to raise children (or otherwise live).

Every time I believe the Holy Spirit is leading me to do something, I'm suddenly bombarded by people who warn me *not to do it!* They're so convincing with their horror stories and worldly wisdom. Usually these people are either beloved relatives or accomplished colleagues.

Isn't it, however, suspicious that they always rush to the scene, and *care so much* about what you do just when you've decided to follow God's lead?

Beware of *ungodly counsel.* When you've decided to be led by the Holy Spirit, know that Satan *will* send people to insist you take another path! How can you tell the difference between godly counsel, wisdom borne from experience, and ungodly counsel?

Examine the lifestyle of the messenger and foundation of the message. Consider the following: Is this messenger led by the Spirit? Do they pray for you before sharing advice? If not led by the Holy Spirit, know that they are extremely vulnerable to being used and led by a darker spirit.

Examine the underlying belief or the origins of their counsel. If the origins are contrary to scripture, the counsel will be ungodly.

Godly counsel will always line up with the entirety of scripture, not just with one or two twisted scriptures. Godly counsel usually comes through a wise, spiritually mature person who lives what they preach and prays for you. Here are examples of other types of counsel:

If Uncle Fred, an unbeliever who builds homes, teaches you to use a level when framing a house, this is probably wisdom borne from experience. As with the rules of gravity, the rules of straight and crooked walls remain the same regardless of morality or spiritual beliefs.

However, if Aunt Martha teaches you that spanking is child abuse and will result in a ruined psyche, this is ungodly counsel. Why? This is the opposite of what the Bible says. Also, the root of this teaching is found in psychology; more specifically, a belief system that says children are mammals not governed by any laws of God (because God does not exist) and we're not under the curse of sin. The belief system assumes that children are born full of goodness and if left to themselves, they will develop into perfectly wonderful beings. Psychology has over 200 contradicting schools of thought, which change constantly – but we'll save that discussion for another book.

We know the Bible teaches that all children are born with a sinful nature, that foolishness is bound up in the heart of a child, and that the rod of discipline will drive it from him, which will save him.

"You, dear children, are from God and have overcome them, because the One who is in you is greater than the one who is in the world. They are from the world and therefore speak from the viewpoint of the world, and the world listens to them. We are from God, and whoever knows God listens to us; but whoever is not from God does not listen to us. This is how we recognize the Spirit of truth and the spirit of falsehood." (1 John 4:4-6 NIV)

Test everything with the Bible as your... well, Bible! The *Sanballats* and *Tobiahs* are very convincing and discouraging, (read the book of Nehemiah for a refresher on these characters), but if we're led by the Holy Spirit, statistics don't apply to us. The Old Testament is filled with illustrations of how God led His people in one miraculous victory after another when they remained faithful and allowed Him to lead.

God *is* in control; therefore, victory doesn't come from our own strength, clever choices, or schemes. We're not defeated by outward influences or circumstances.

"At that time Hanani the seer came to Asa king of Judah and said to him: 'Because you relied on the king of Aram and not on the LORD your God, the army of the king of Aram has escaped from your hand. Were not the Cushites and Libyans a mighty army with great numbers of chariots and horsemen? Yet when you relied on the LORD, he delivered them into your hand. For the eyes of the LORD range throughout the earth to strengthen those whose hearts are fully committed to him. You have done a foolish thing, and from now on you will be at war.'" (2 Chronicles 16:7-9 NIV)

We're defeated when we follow the ways of the nations and ungodly cultures around us. If we condone sin within our lives, or put our hope in something or someone other than our Lord, He will allow us to be defeated.

"But the Israelites acted unfaithfully in regard to the devoted things; Achan son of Carmi, the son of Zimri, the son of Zerah, of the tribe of Judah, took some of them. So the LORD's anger burned against Israel.
Now Joshua sent men from Jericho to Ai, which is near Beth Aven to the east of Bethel, and told them, 'Go up and spy out the region.' So the men went up and spied out Ai.

"When they returned to Joshua, they said, 'Not all the people will have to go up against Ai. Send two or three thousand men to take it and do not weary all the people, for only a few men are there.' So about three thousand men went up; but they were routed by the men of Ai, who killed about thirty-six of them. They chased the Israelites from the city gate as far as the stone quarries and struck them down on the slopes. At this the hearts of the people melted and became like water.

"Then Joshua tore his clothes and fell facedown to the ground before the ark of the LORD, remaining there till evening. The elders of Israel did the same, and sprinkled dust on their heads. And Joshua said, 'Ah, Sovereign LORD, why did you ever bring this people across the Jordan to deliver us into the hands of the Amorites to destroy us? If only we had been content to stay on the other side of the Jordan! O Lord, what can I say, now that Israel has been routed by its enemies? The Canaanites and the other people of the country will hear about this and they will surround us and wipe out our name from the earth. What then will you do for your own great name?'

"The LORD said to Joshua, 'Stand up! What are you doing down on your face? Israel has sinned; they have violated my covenant, which I commanded them to keep. They have taken some of the devoted things; they have stolen, they have lied, they have put them with their own possessions. That is why the Israelites cannot stand against their enemies; they turn their backs and run because they have been made liable to destruction. I will not be with you anymore unless you destroy whatever among you is devoted to destruction.

"Go, consecrate the people. Tell them, ' Consecrate yourselves in preparation for tomorrow; for this is what the LORD, the God of Israel, says: That which is devoted is among you, O Israel. *You cannot stand against your enemies until you remove it.*'" (Joshua 7:1-13 NIV)

3

Harnessing Your Big Heart

If you've read this far, congratulations; I assume you understand you're in a spiritual battle for souls, or you're at least humoring me and my opinions.

I also assume other things about you: You have a *very* big heart. You love kids. You trust in Jesus and you're praying to be used to enrich the lives of others, saving those who can be saved and so forth.

But please take a moment to realize that however mature you might be in your faith (it might be a healthful, large faith; and if so, good for you!) you're still new to fostering or adopting.

One of the first things you must understand is that the vast majority of adoptable children have lasting developmental, psychological, or emotional disabilities and challenges. Yes, even the healthy ones.

Whether abused, neglected, or even if you adopt an infant, most have permanent damage because their birth mothers drank alcohol or used drugs during pregnancy. It's quite natural for a parent to love and protect their children, so when that doesn't happen, substance abuse is usually in-volved. While extreme poverty, domestic violence, inherited mental illness or learning disabilities sometimes play a big role in a parent's inability to care for children, in most of those cases you'll still see alcohol and drug abuse. Therefore, all parents considering adoption should understand what maternal alcohol and drug usage do to a developing infant.

Much of the information in this book applies to the children labeled as "healthy" by the adoption agencies. If a child *has* already been labeled with a disability, they're exhibiting obvious, pronounced symptoms. Most children who go through the adoption system are either too young or too transient (haven't been with one caregiver long) to be accu-rately evaluated. Therefore, *a majority of the children adopted out as "perfectly healthy" will manifest some of these disabilities and challenges* (discussed in further chapters) *as you live with them.*

For this reason, go slowly. Don't jump in the deep end before you can swim; don't bite off more than you can chew... and any other clichés that might apply.

During my first year as a foster parent, I had a strong desire to adopt a six-year-old girl who was diagnosed with RAD (Reactive Attachment Disorder). She lived in a shelter be-cause she was too troubled and disruptive to be in a foster home. She spent a long time in the shelter before they even classified her as "ready to adopt." She was a damaged child with many serious emotional and behavioral issues.

Naturally, this information didn't scare me; it increased my desire to save her. However, at this time my oldest biological daughter was about seven years old and my younger kids were... well, younger than six years old.

Thank God, I had a seasoned and wise licensing worker. She told me that I wasn't ready to take such a hard case. I argued; she argued back. She cautioned that bringing in a difficult child of that age would upset the whole order of things in my family. The girl was older than my youngest children, so she would become the leader. Instead of my loving children being the examples, the troubled child would exert the peer pressure. Because my children were younger, they'd be vulnerable to abuse; they would look up to her and follow her example.

In the end, after much prayer I conceded that perhaps my licensing worker was right. Now, years later, I could kiss her for that advice. I know, without a doubt, that it would have been a tragic and lasting mistake.

Mistakes happen, but once you adopt... what do you do if you realize you've goofed and your family is suffering?

Many adoptions disrupt each year (the children are given back to the child welfare system or a private agency), but as a big-hearted person with more faith than experience, you probably wouldn't quit on this child; even if you were losing your sanity and your family were falling apart. So slow down, read on, and let's be sure you're prepared before you commit.

Why do dogs bark? Why do cats meow? Isn't it because it's part of their *nature*? Now read this and then tell me what behaviors originate from the sinful *nature* (with which all people are born):

"So I say, live by the Spirit, and you will not gratify the desires of the sinful nature. For the sinful nature desires what is contrary to the Spirit, and the Spirit what is contrary to the sinful nature. They are in conflict with each other, so that you do not do what you want. But if you are led by the Spirit, you are not under law.

"The acts of the sinful nature are obvious: sexual immorality, impurity and debauchery; idolatry and witchcraft; hatred, discord, jealousy, fits of rage, selfish ambition, dissensions, factions and envy; drunkenness, orgies, and the like. I warn you, as I did before, that those who live like this will not inherit the kingdom of God.

"But the fruit of the Spirit is love, joy, peace, patience, kindness, goodness, faithfulness, gentleness and self-control. Against such things there is no law. Those who belong to Christ Jesus have crucified the sinful nature with its passions and desires. Since we live by the Spirit, let us keep in step with the Spirit. Let us not become conceited, provoking and envying each other." (Galatians 5:16-26 NIV)

When you plan to adopt, you'll be given a checklist of behaviors and disabilities. You'll mark this paper up like a Christmas wish list, naming the disabilities and behaviors that you'll consider and those you absolutely will not consider.

Defiant? Okay, I guess.
Fire-starter? No way.
Needs medication? Okay, sure, why not?
Sexually abuses other children? Absolutely not!

There's nothing wrong with being selective; this is your family and you're responsible for controlling the environment and you know there are some things just too difficult for you to handle. But guess what? If you adopt any child who hasn't been born again, who is not indwelt by and *led by the Holy Spirit of God*, that child is still *only natural*; they are, as all unbelievers, blind to spiritual things and ruled by their *sinful nature*. So, even if they've never been abused, never been exposed to evil things, *if they lack normal inhibitions and have poor impulse control* (as most needy children do), what behaviors will you likely see?

Sexual immorality, impurity and debauchery; idolatry and witchcraft; hatred, discord, jealousy, fits of rage, selfish ambition, dissensions, factions and envy; drunkenness, orgies, and the like.

Are you prepared to deal with these behaviors *in your home?*

Even if you were promised a perfect child, without behaviors, this is the *natural* (sinful) core of each human. Every child has the potential to act out. *Every child or adult*, due to a sinful nature, has the potential to become violent, lie, steal, start fires, or molest others, etc.

But a child who *lacks normal inhibitions and impulse control* will almost definitely act out in these ways rather than controlling their urges.

Do you understand what I'm saying? I'm trying to be gentle, but countless adoptions are dissolved (or disrupted) each year because the adopted child has behaviors that are so disturbing or harmful that the family feels it cannot survive, or the child cannot survive, unless they're removed – *un*-adopted. Other adoptive families are still trying to make it work, but paying "therapeutic" ranches and other facilities to care for their child. This can easily cost $3,000 to $10,000 monthly, but they see no other option; they cannot safely keep their adopted child in their home.

Enter every single case of adoption or fostercare prepared, expecting and guarding against these behaviors so they'll not injure the child or anyone else. For this reason, it's usually *extremely unwise* to bring a child into your home that's older than (or the same age as) your youngest child. Guard the children you've already been given to protect!

THINGS TO REMEMBER:

The following are guidelines I set for myself when bringing a new child into my home through the fostercare system. If you're going straight to adoption, then glean what you can from these and apply however they fit:

1. You're not as invincible as you think.

2. You're not even half as invincible as you think.

3. Remember your priorities; your relationship with Jesus comes first, of course, but next is your marriage (if you're married). If at any time you have a child-placement (or *any* situation) that's causing your marital relationship to break down, seriously consider having the child moved elsewhere or get out of the situation. If your marital relationship is breaking down because of this child, realize that God will prepare the right home for that child, and *you are not it.* Without a strong marriage, you're not giving your children (or any child) the safe haven they need. Take a look at the statistics regarding children who grow up fatherless or in single-parent homes; it's not pretty. There's an enormous gap

between how those children fare compared with those who grow up in two-parent homes.

4. Remember that after your commitment to keeping your marriage healthful, your existing children are your next priority above anyone else you might want to save or help. If you've taken a child-placement (or put yourself into *any* situation) that's threatening the well-being or emotional or spiritual safety of your existing children, please do the right thing and get out of that situation. If it's a child-placement, have the child moved to another home. Pray that God will provide the right home. Realize that *if you were it*, things would've worked out.

5. Remember when bringing in a new child, begin as you want to continue! Do not coddle or indulge the child; they're probably accustomed to different rules or none at all. Establish the rules of your home (kindly, but consistently) and begin to train them to fit in. Do not compromise! Expect to live with the child for two weeks before making a decision. In my experience, by the time two weeks have passed, things have settled and calmed down, or I know it isn't going to work. (Naturally, if you have a really bad situation, bail earlier.) You're only *part of* the system. Don't be prideful; every child is *not* intended for you. *If you're the one* God has called to do the job, it will work without damaging your family or your loved ones.

6. Remember numbers one and two above. If at any time you feel your sanity or ability to be a *safe* parent is doubtful, pray and ask God to show you a way to remedy the situation. If you're still floundering, don't feel guilty; have the child removed immediately. *(This applies to foster children – the*

process is more complicated for adopted children). Never allow yourself to become stressed to the point of being ready to lose control. If that happens, you really will be guilty. Do what you must to keep the peace in your home and to have *no regrets.*

7. Remember that there's no such thing as a truly "well adjusted" non-believer. Yes, some repress their destructive urges and some are just really good at hiding their bad behaviors. Some are so good at repressing destructive urges or hiding bad behaviors that they're quite successful *in this life.* So what?

What does it profit a man if he gains the whole world, yet loses his soul? *Your main goal is not to raise well-adjusted children, but rather to bring the life-changing message of the Gospel to lost souls.* If you work with a troubled, damaged child and he never becomes a successful or productive citizen, but he believes the Gospel and has a saving faith in Jesus Christ, you have succeeded. Adoption is a ministry to unsaved souls.

Be in prayer and read the scriptures daily, asking God to guide you. Be led by the Holy Spirit, not by your feelings *or your big heart.*

4

Trading In Your Toad

For the Sake of the Children?

Authors note: I wrote Trading in your Toad in 2001 as an assignment for writing class. For smoother reading, I compiled the personalities of my two sons into one character and called him Caleb. That probably wasn't fair; Caleb owned the big brown eyes, but the cowlick, grin and misfired baseballs belonged to Corban.

While this article doesn't specifically address adoption, I believe the information here can benefit anyone attempting to parent a child. An intact marriage is vital to the well-being of your children. Guard yours at all costs.

Caleb turned seven years old this year. Seems like just yesterday I counted his fingers and toes, held him to my chest and breathed in that new baby smell. Sometimes I wonder what grew faster: Caleb or my love for him.

He has this cowlick that won't lie down, an impish grin and a habit of pulling the cat's tail. He misfires his baseball through my windows, wipes chocolate on my couch, and he even overshoots the toilet; but when he turns those big brown eyes on me, I'm wrapped around his little finger.

Sometimes I catch myself watching him do something, thinking, "Oh how cute!" and then I stop. I realize that if he weren't mine, I'd probably be thinking, "What a brat!"

Maybe you're different, but for most of us, patient love comes easier for our own children. I'd like to say that's just my opinion, but it's not. The statistics sadly agree.

This year, one million American kids will become the newest casualties of divorce. Their parents will divorce to escape the stress of a loveless marriage, the strife of having irreconcilable differences, or to ease the heartache of betrayal. They might divorce *for the sake of the children*. Many parents who divorce assume that living within the confines of a miserable marriage is more harmful to their children, but statistics say in most cases they're dead wrong.

Take John and Jane for example:
John met Jane (not their real names, of course) and they fell in love. Maybe they knew that fifty-percent of first marriages end in divorce, maybe they didn't. Either way, they were happy and hopeful when they said their vows.

Before their first anniversary, Jane was pregnant and John was looking for a better paying job. It wasn't easy, but eventually they got the house, new car, and a Golden Retriever puppy for their bouncing baby boy, Bobby.

Baby number two, Susie, came along a couple of years later and they bought her a Siamese kitten. If they were exactly like the average statistical family, they'd have only one-and-a-half children. Fortunately, this couple had a whole second child!

John and Jane tried for awhile to make things work, but life was hard. Heart-pounding love is the most fragile of all diseases and as they both grew and changed, they were cured. (She grew a bit of a mustache and his chest began to sag, but possibly that's neither here nor there.) Their relationship wasn't exceedingly violent (they were never featured on COPS), but water under the bridge rose and eventually they wondered why they ever got married. In their eleventh year of marriage, they surrendered to irreconcilable differences.

They split the children, the dog, the cat, and their belongings; it was quite messy really, not to mention expensive.

After a yearlong tug-o-war, Jane got primary custody of the children and John got visitation. All things considered, theirs was a peaceful parting. They remained friends of a sort, but sold off the house and belongings that they won from each other (too many bad memories) and lost the cat and dog in the shuffle. For a time, they vowed to avoid the opposite sex forever.

All too soon, they were lonely and found themselves with new partners. (Incidentally, their new partners were someone else's old partners...) Naturally, they all got new homes, new cars, and a new dog and cat for each family. (John got a German Shepherd and a Persian; Jane got a Cocker Spaniel and a moggy.) John and Jane were in love (with their new partners) and optimistic. The best things were yet to come.

Like most couples, they hadn't intended to divorce and remarry, but life seldom mimics our ideals. By now, John and Jane knew something of statistics: they knew that 60% of remarriages end in divorce and some nasty realities abound in life after divorce. However, if 60% end in another divorce, that leaves 40%. John and Jane hoped they'd be in that number.

Things may have been different if Jane had known that sexual abuse by stepfathers is five times higher than among natural fathers. For Susie's sake, someone should have told them that the most common age for onset of this abuse is age 10; at least then, Jane could have taken precautions.

Susie turned 10 the year after Jane remarried, right around the time that Jane was starting to wonder why she married her new husband and he was feeling her rejection...

Within a few years, Jane was divorced again, struggling to pay the bills, trying to keep her new boyfriend and Bobbie from each other's throats, and she couldn't control Susie. (Susie was making horrible allegations against her ex-stepfather, but Bobby (being a boy) wasn't talking.)

John had his own life to worry about; his newest ex-wife was causing him grief. He now had children with her as well, and both ex-wives were demanding child-support. Eventually, he moved in with a girlfriend for financial purposes. Bobby and Susie didn't get along with Dad's new girlfriend, so they didn't see him often. They were both having trouble in school. Before Susie reached high school, she ran away from home numerous times and her brother was in trouble with the law.

Before they turned eighteen, Bobbie dropped out of school and attempted suicide and Susie got pregnant. Need I even mention how many dogs and cats they went through?

Their lives would have made a great soap opera. Unfortunately, statistics say they were traveling right in step with the majority. Fatherless homes account for 90% of homeless/runaway children, 85% of children with behavior problems, 71% of high school dropouts, 85% of youths in prison, well over 50% of teen mothers, and 63% of youth suicides. *(1)*

If Bobbie and Susie make it to adulthood and decide to marry, they'll be 50% more likely to get divorced than their counterparts from intact families.

It's like the song that never ends... and John and Jane still say they divorced *for the sake of the children.*

I understand that they tried to make things work, then believed they'd end the strife by divorcing, but if I believe I can fly, that won't make it so. They had good intentions; even resolved to stay single unless they found an excellent mate -- one who made them feel better about themselves and who spent quality time with their children -- who wasn't such a toad. But people get lonely waiting for princes.

Nobody, no matter how princely they are, will ever see Bobby and Susie with their parents' eyes.

Likewise, no one will ever view my son Caleb with my heart. No one but his own father will have that supernatural, beyond- explaining connection with him. If anyone on earth is capable of putting up with his idiosyncrasies as he grows, we, his parents, have the best shot.

By no means do divorce and remarriage always end up on the

wrong end of the statistics. Neither are they the ultimate culprits of child abuse and neglect, but they are contributing factors to the usual suspects.

Consider that 45% of women experience a drop in their standard of living after divorce. (2) The findings of the National Center on Child Abuse and Neglect's NIH (National Incidence) 1993 study clearly say that the overall rate of maltreatment (abuse and neglect combined) in the United States was lowest in families with incomes above $30,000 per year; 10 times higher in families with incomes between $15,000 and $30,000 per year; and 22 times higher for families with incomes below $15,000 per year. (3)

Other strongly implicated family characteristics that contribute to abuse risk were single parent status, substance abusing parents, and large family size. (4) In addition, cohabitation is a major factor in child abuse. The evidence suggests that a lack of commitment between biological parents is dangerous for children, and that a lack of commitment between mother and boyfriend is exceedingly dangerous. The risk of child abuse is 20 times higher than in traditional married families if biological parents are cohabiting (as in "common law" marriages) and 33 times higher if the single mother is cohabiting with a boyfriend (not related to her children). (1)

How rampant a problem is child abuse and neglect? Compare it with other known dangers and you'll see:

> * Each year an average of 17 people die from attacks by dogs (most fatalities are children) and 30 different breeds are responsible. (5) (Despite the breed variations, our media is ever diligent in exclaiming the dangers of certain breeds of dogs.)

* Another danger to children are car air-bags: 67 children died in automobile crashes involving air bags between 1993 and 1997 and the result was mass awareness of this danger.

However, did anyone tell you that during the same five-year period, nearly 5,000 children died from abuse or neglect at the hands of the parent or guardian responsible for their care? Did you know that approximately 15 million children were victims of abuse or serious neglect during this time? (2)

Child abuse is definitely a clear and present danger. A home life with two biological parents is far and away the safest environment for a child. (6)

Yes, Caleb turned seven this year -- with happiness that he never tries to hide and an innocence that comes from never tasting serious heartache. He has a dog and a cat, a brother and two sisters; but most of all, he has us, his parents.

Has my husband always been a prince in my eyes? Take a wild guess. Caleb doesn't know how many times we've both been tempted to run (not walk) away from marriage. He doesn't need to know.

At his age, he doesn't need to know that marriage is a gazillion times harder than I'd expected. I'm not going to tell him that sometimes I think his dad is a toad of the highest order. But when he's older, I'll sit him down and explain that divorce and remarriage is usually just a matter of trading in one old toad for another.

We've come a long way, baby, but Grandma was wiser than we knew.

Staying together for the children isn't as simpleminded as we once believed. Does your husband beat you up? murder your pets? sexually molest the children? *If not*, then he's worth a second look -- perhaps he's not as big a toad as you think.

Maybe -- with prayer and hard work -- if you stay together and toil as you would toward any other worthy goal, you can rekindle the friendship that drew you together in the beginning.

It's worth another try -- *for the sake of the children.*

1.   www.childabuse.com/perp.htm, "Why Child Abuse Occurs & the   common criminal background of the abuser"

2.   http://www.divorcemag.com/, U.S.A Divorce Statistics, 1997

3.   Sedlak and Broadhurst, Third National Incidence Study of Child   Abuse and Neglect, p. 53

4.   www.childabuse.com/ taken from National Center on Child Abuse   and Neglect's National Incidence Study, 1993 by Westat Associates.

5.   www.dogbitelaw.com, statistics since 1975

6.   Whelan, Broken Homes & Battered Children.

Part Two:

The

Adoptable

Children

Letter to a junkie:

I don't know your name, though I may have seen your face. Sometimes I take a wrong turn and cruise by the rumpled people sleeping in Tucson's alleys and that place we call Needle Park. I'd call you if I could or send a card -- message in a bottle - whatever it took, but I can't.

You didn't leave your name.

So, Mr. Anonymous Junkie, who wasn't at the crack house anymore when the cops answered your call, thank you. I've a button-nosed toddler here who owes you her life. She's my foster daughter, but not for long. Soon I'll sign adoption papers and she'll wear my name. She already has my heart. My chubby, little girl who loves to read books and draw pictures of kittens; kittens in bright pinks, greens, and smiling yellow. However, she wasn't that way when you saved her.

"I never did this before," you said when you called 911, "but there's a kid over here, a baby. You got to come for her." Since children might read this letter, I won't repeat what you said your buddy was doing to her... thinking about it makes my gut burn and fists clench, so I try not to think about it. I pray she'll have an easier time forgetting. Even though you weren't in your right mind, you knew enough to make the call.

"We partied with her mom," you said, "then she took off with another dude, left the baby here. Says she'll be right back, like, days ago. We're messed up; babies don't need this life."

I want you to know she's doing much better now. She doesn't always have that terrified, wild animal look anymore -- sometimes, yes, but not all the time. It's been months since the last time I found her digging through the trash looking for something to eat. She's learning to trust, trying to play. The monsoon storms terrified her at first, but we held hands while the thunder bellowed and then we played in the rain. Well, I played. She watched, then splashed with hesitation for awhile, but later she smiled. Eventually she even laughed; it was beautiful.

Because of what you did, she's going to be okay.

A lot of people say, "I'm no saint," like that's their excuse. They could learn a lesson from you, Sir. Nobody's so far gone that God can't use them for good. If they're still soft enough to hear that voice - you know, the silent one that screams when something's not right, "Help that person!" - then they can do something about it.

That's all I wanted to say, really. I'm just sitting here while the cool night falls over the desert and the clouds are black as sin. I've a fire in the hearth, my feet up on the couch, and a sweet toddler tucked into my lap. We're sitting here thinking of you. Thanking God for you. Knowing your life would probably be different if someone had picked up the phone, got you some help when you were little. We're wondering where you are tonight.

The rain's coming down now.

5

God's Children

Happy, *successful* adoptions of healthy, emotionally stable children definitely are a reality. In these adoptions, both child and adoptive parents immediately sprout a deep and abiding bond for the other; their parenting challenges are no different from that of any biological parent. This book focuses more on adopting *the difficult (or troubled) child*; however, it also gives you a *better chance* of choosing the less difficult, if that's what you wish. By knowing circumstances of which to be aware before you adopt, you're prepared to make informed choices. The following could be considered *green* flags:

* The child is adopted young (an infant or toddler).

* If not an infant, the child has been lovingly nurtured from the moment of birth; they have a bond to their caregiver. (Child was not in an institution with changing/rotating employees; was not transient with multiple, temporary care givers.)

* The child's needs were always met; they never felt the need to protect themselves or fight to survive.

* The child's biological parents did not have inherited mental illness, mental deficit, or severe emotional instability.

* The baby did not suffer any prenatal exposure to alcohol or drugs.

If the adoptable child fits *all of the above* green flags, the outlook is very positive. For example:

> If a young, but stable/intelligent, healthy mother (non-drinker, non-smoker, etc.) gives up a child (at birth) simply because she doesn't feel ready to raise a baby, the outlook for that child is very good.
> OR
> If you adopt from a country that has little to no substance abuse problem, and if the baby has one-on-one love and nurturing from the moment of birth until they're put in your arms, problems will likely be minimal.

But for children born into other situations, they and their adoptive parents should prepare for challenges above and beyond those of typical parenting.

Armed with that information, prayerfully consider where you fit in to adoption. Each has his gift. Jesus is the savior of the world – not me; not you. We're each pieces of Christ's body and when working together, form a whole.

For those who adopt difficult children (whether by choice or through ignorance), we know we need help raising them, and that God will give the Holy Spirit to all who ask. When faced with extremely troubling behaviors, remember that God adopted you also, and you were probably not the cream of the crop.

> "For the foolishness of God is wiser than man's wisdom, and the weakness of God is stronger than man's strength.

"Brothers, think of what you were when you were called. Not many of you were wise by human standards; not many were influential; not many were of noble birth. But God chose the foolish things of the world to shame the wise; God chose the weak things of the world to shame the strong. He chose the lowly things of this world and the despised things—and the things that are not—to nullify the things that are, so that no one may boast before him. It is because of him that you are in Christ Jesus, who has become for us wisdom from God—that is, our righteousness, holiness and redemption. Therefore, as it is written: 'Let him who boasts boast in the Lord.'" (1 Corinthians 1:25-31 NIV)

Learn to see adoption as spiritual or *evangelism.*

I'm always amazed at how many of the believers that I know were first exposed to the Gospel (and believed wholeheartedly) as children. For most of us, our faith didn't become life-changing until we were adults. We forgot Jesus for awhile, but He remembered us. God remained faithful, kept us *set apart*, and *called us back* to Him.

This is my prayer for the children that God lets me hold in my arms.

How much impact do you have on the people around you?

Please read the entire story of Paul's shipwreck in Acts, Chapter 27. Take special notice of this:

"Last night an angel of the God whose I am and whom I serve stood beside me and said, 'Do not be afraid, Paul. You must stand trial before Caesar; and God has graciously *given you the lives* of all who sail with you.'" (Acts 27:23-24 NIV)

Paul describes himself as one who both *serves* and *belongs to* God; if this also describes *you*, then ask God to *give you the lives of the children who* "*sail with you.*" We live in a world of storms that are driving the lives of many toward shipwreck; countless souls are lost in the sea of sin. When God places any child in my arms (even if only overnight as foster mommy) I pray He'll see this child as mine in the spirit world and set them apart for salvation.

What about the *sins of the fathers* being visited upon their children?

In ancient times, God described Himself this way:

> "... I, the LORD your God, am a jealous God, punishing the children for the sin of the fathers to the third and fourth genera- tion of those who hate me..." (Exodus 20:5 NIV)

This is often quoted to prove that children are destined to repeat the sins of their parents, but to understand Exodus 20:5, you need more information. First of all, God made that promise as part of His covenant with the Israelites. If the child is not an Israelite (or Jewish) by birth, or has never officially converted to Judaism, they're automatically *exclud- ed* from any covenants made in the Old Testament with the Israelites. In other words, if the law (the Ten Command- ments, etc.) is all we have, then we and our children are already outside of God's favor, if we're gentiles. Thankfully, God's interaction with man didn't stop at the covenant He made with the Israelites there; He later tells them this:

> "In those days people will no longer say, 'The fathers have eaten sour grapes, and the children's teeth are set on edge.' Instead,

everyone will die for his own sin; whoever eats sour grapes—his own teeth will be set on edge.

"'The time is coming,' declares the LORD, 'when I will make a new covenant with the house of Israel and with the house of Judah.
It will not be like the covenant I made with their forefathers when I took them by the hand to lead them out of Egypt, because they broke my covenant, though I was a husband to them,' declares the LORD.

"'This is the covenant I will make with the house of Israel after that time,' declares the LORD. 'I will put my law in their minds and write it on their hearts. I will be their God, and they will be my people.

"No longer will a man teach his neighbor, or a man his brother, saying, 'Know the LORD,' because they will all know me, from the least of them to the greatest,' declares the LORD. 'For I will forgive their wickedness and will remember their sins no more.'"
(Jeremiah 31:29-34 NIV)

It's evident here, and in the New Testament, that God has a plan to set people free from the condemnation the Ten Commandments prove we deserve. Again in Ezekiel, He addresses the idea of children *not* being punished for their father's sins:

"The word of the LORD came to me: 'What do you people mean by quoting this proverb about the land of Israel:

"The fathers eat sour grapes, and the children's teeth are set on edge?'

"'As surely as I live,' declares the Sovereign LORD, 'You will no longer quote this proverb in Israel. For every living soul belongs to me, the father as well as the son—both alike belong to me. The soul who sins is the one who will die.

"Suppose there is a righteous man who does what is just and right. He does not eat at the mountain shrines or look to the idols of the house of Israel. He does not defile his neighbor's wife or lie with a woman during her period. He does not oppress anyone, but returns what he took in pledge for a loan. He does not commit robbery but gives his food to the hungry and provides clothing for the naked. He does not lend at usury or take excessive interest. He withholds his hand from doing wrong and judges fairly between man and man. He follows my decrees and faithfully keeps my laws. That man is righteous; he will surely live,' declares the Sovereign LORD.

"'Suppose he has a violent son, who sheds blood or does any of these other things' (though the father has done none of them): 'He eats at the mountain shrines. He defiles his neighbor's wife. He oppresses the poor and needy. He commits robbery. He does not return what he took in pledge. He looks to the idols. He does detestable things. He lends at usury and takes excessive interest. Will such a man live? He will not! Because he has done all these detestable things, he will surely be put to death and his blood will be on his own head.

"But suppose this son has a son who sees all the sins his father commits, and though he sees them, he does not do such things: "He does not eat at the mountain shrines or look to the idols of the house of Israel. He does not defile his neighbor's wife. He does not oppress anyone or require a pledge for a loan. He does not commit robbery but gives his food to the hungry and provides clothing for the naked. He withholds his hand from sin and takes no usury or excessive interest. He keeps my laws and follows my decrees. He will not die for his father's sin; he will surely live. But his father will die for his own sin, because he practiced extortion, robbed his brother and did what was wrong among his people.

"Yet you ask, 'Why does the son not share the guilt of his father?' Since the son has done what is just and right and has been careful to keep all my decrees, he will surely live. The soul who sins is the one who will die. The son will not share the guilt of the father, nor will the father share the guilt of the son. The righteousness of the righteous man will be credited to him, and the wickedness of the wicked will be charged against him.

"But if a wicked man turns away from all the sins he has committed and keeps all my decrees and does what is just and right, he will surely live; he will not die.'"(Ezekiel 18:1-21 NIV)

As believers in Christ, we're under a new covenant that is different from what you read in Ezekiel and different from the covenant God made with the Israelites when he brought them out of Egypt, but these scriptures show us God's heart. He longs to see our adopted children (and us) free from sin and forgiven. Peter, when addressing Jewish believers (some who were saying the gentiles must keep the Law of Moses in order to be saved), said this:

"Now then, why do you try to test God by putting on the necks of the disciples a yoke that neither we nor our fathers have been able to bear? No! We believe it is through the grace of our Lord Jesus that we are saved, just as they are." (Acts 15:10-11 NIV)

Therefore, my goal as an adoptive mother is to bring the children into a relationship with Christ so that they're adopted by Him as well and clothed in Christ's righteousness.

"Praise be to the God and Father of our Lord Jesus Christ, who has blessed us in the heavenly realms with every spiritual blessing in Christ. For he chose us in him before the creation of the world to be holy and blameless in his sight.

In love he predestined us to be adopted as his sons through Jesus Christ, in accordance with his pleasure and will— to the praise of his glorious grace, which he has freely given us in the One he loves. In him we have redemption through his blood, the forgiveness of sins, in accordance with the riches of God's grace that he lavished on us with all wisdom and understanding." (Ephesians 1:3-8 NIV)

However, I'm convinced that even before believing the Gospel, they come under sanctification simply because I've held them in my arms as *my children*. Yes, everyone is responsible for his or her own sins, but God "sets apart" those who live with a believer that fervently seeks God on their behalf. Or, as we saw earlier, 275 people were saved from shipwreck simply because they *sailed with* Paul!

In 1 Corinthians, Chapter 7, we see that an unbelieving spouse is set apart, or sanctified, in God's eyes simply by remaining with his *believing spouse*. The result, it says, is that the *children are holy*. Likewise, Abraham's children automatically received the covenant when *Abraham believed* God and was counted as righteous.

"Therefore, the promise comes by faith, so that it may be by grace and may be guaranteed to all Abraham's offspring—not only to those who are of the law but also to those who are of the faith of Abraham. He is the father of us all. As it is written: "I have made you a father of many nations." He is our father in the sight of God, in whom he believed—the God who gives life to the dead and calls things that are not as though they were." (Romans 4:16-17 NIV)

I don't claim to totally understand these things, but evidence is overwhelming in scripture that "parentage" does not necessarily mean biological or "blood," -- and God saves others for *your sake if you serve and belong to Him.*

> "So when God destroyed the cities of the plain, he remembered Abraham, and he brought Lot out of the catastrophe that overthrew the cities where Lot had lived." (Genesis 19:29 NIV)

Why did God save Lot from the destruction? Because God "remembered Abraham." *In Genesis, Chapters 11 and 12, we learn that Lot was orphaned, or at least fatherless, and was taken in first by his grandfather and then later by his uncle Abraham.*

☼pen adoption verses closed adoption?

If you don't know the basics of open adoption and closed adoption, please review the Glossary. When comparing the two, it's impossible to say one is better than the other; there are positives and negatives to both and so many variables.

Whichever you choose, determine to put no stumbling block before these little ones. A stumbling block can be offering too much information before they can comprehend, or too little when they can. I see parents operating in both extremes; I caution you to pray over this area and be sensitive to God's direction.

Regarding "too much information too early," I often see children lose all sense of security and hope of having a happy, normal childhood because parents want to discuss everything *now.*

There are many subjects a child isn't capable of understanding; to force it confuses and worries her. For a child, the love and security of being part of a family (as nature intended) are vital to her emotional health as she grows. Be sensitive and patient; give your child the most normal childhood possible under the circumstances. Don't help Satan erode your child's sense of security by baffling her.

On the other end of the spectrum are those who simply cannot tell the truth, ever; avoid this as well. When your child is mentally and emotionally ready to talk about biological matters, be honest. Don't promise him that his biological parents were wonderful people who loved him and had his best interests at heart when placing him up for adoption. Sure, that may have been their calculated motive, but (usually) if they'd been living the pure and circumspect, unselfish lives God intended for them, they could've given the child a stable family environment in which to grow up.

But won't those facts make your child feel badly about himself?

You can hope so! The heart of the Gospel is man coming to terms with his inner depravity and lack of redeemable qualities. He needs forgiveness, needs to be clothed with Christ's righteousness, and needs to be filled with God's Holy Spirit – but he won't ask if he doesn't understand his need! Give your child the truth: his biological parents were sinners, just as we all are.

> "But God demonstrates his own love for us in this: While we were still sinners, Christ died for us." (Romans 5:8 NIV)

Usually, the sin of the biological parents rendered them incapable (or unwilling) to spend their lives nurturing a child. If you don't allow your child to accept this fact, how will he face his own sinful nature and necessity to "die to himself" and let Christ live through him?

Your child needs to understand that you chose to put aside your selfish ambitions and nurture him. When he was without love in the world, you brought him into your heart and arms; you gave him your life, your family, and your name to call his own regardless of whether he ever gave anything back. When your child understands this truth, it may help him to see God's heart toward him; it will give him an example of true love that he can follow.

What about preserving cultural roots?

If you spend time in "adoption circles," you'll learn that it's popular these days to raise adopted children with constant reminders of their biological past. Adoptive parents incorporate cultural or ethnic traditions into the family, and sometimes even create "life books" chronicling the child's pre-adoption history.

I believe these practices can be harmful in many instances. I'll explain – but first, read these scriptures and consider where each child *really* came from:

> "For you created my inmost being; you knit me together in my mother's womb. I praise you because I am fearfully and wonderfully made; your works are wonderful, I know that full well." (Psalm 139:13-14 NIV)

> "'For in him we live and move and have our being.' As some of your own poets have said, 'We are his offspring.' Therefore since *we are God's offspring*, we should not think that the divine being is like gold or silver or stone—an image made by man's design and skill." (Acts 17:28-29 NIV)

> "Do you not know that your bodies are members of Christ himself?"

> "Do you not know that *your body is a temple* of the Holy Spirit, who is in you, whom you have received from God? You are not your own; you were bought at a price. Therefore honor God with your body." (1 Corinthians 6:15, 19-20 NIV)

In scripture, it's clear that God carefully created our bodies (or our adopted children's bodies!) and that they were made *for Him*. Our bodies are called "tents" in scripture; they're only temporary dwellings, but the implication isn't that of an old, tattered camping tent. The original wording suggests something more dignified, similar to the *"Tent of Meeting"* you find in Israel's history. Scripture suggests that the Tent of Meeting (a place where God would meet with man) was a reflection of the Temple (later built by Solomon) and that temple was a reflection of what we'll find in heaven. If you're following me, the point is that our bodies were created to be filled with God's Holy Spirit; a place where we could commune with God. They're a shadow of the bodies we'll have when we're fully in the presence of God in heaven and they are, in God's eyes, his *temple*. Regardless of where your child was born or into which situation, the reason God created her was to be H*is child*, walking in friendship with Him and being filled with His Holy Spirit and love.

This is my first concern with any "life books" which remind the child of a painful history or emphasize their biologically cultural ties; *we are not of this world!*

> "I have given them your word and the world has hated them, for they are not of the world any more than I am of the world." (John 17:14 NIV)

Our children shouldn't find their identity in their physical bodies. If we are only a physical being, we have no hope of resurrection and no hope of being anyone apart from this temporary body. When this body dies, we would cease to exist. In addition, much of the history, cultures or ethnic traditions your adopted child might be *biologically tied to*, stem from sin or idolatrous religions.

Will God be pleased if He redeems a child from this evil and bondage and then her adoptive parents try to put her back in to it? No, your adopted child is not just a physical body whose origins began with two humans or a race of people. *Your adopted child has history prior to birth or even conception* – when she was inside God's imagination and then His hands as He decided to *fearfully and wonderfully* knit her together; teach your child *this heritage*. Give your child a "life book" that ties her to her creator, not to the sins of biological ancestors.

> "Sing to God, sing praise to his name, extol him who rides on the clouds — his name is the LORD — and rejoice before him. A father to the fatherless, a defender of widows, is God in his holy dwelling. God sets the lonely in families, he leads forth the prisoners with singing; but the rebellious live in a sun-scorched land." (Psalm 68:4-6 NIV)

> "Religion that God our Father accepts as pure and faultless is this: to look after orphans and widows in their distress and to keep oneself from being polluted by the world." (James 1:27 NIV)

> "For the LORD your God is God of gods and Lord of lords, the great God, mighty and awesome, who shows no partiality and accepts no bribes. He defends the cause of the fatherless and the

widow, and loves the alien, giving him food and clothing."
(Deuteronomy 10:17-18 NIV)

"Defend the cause of the weak and fatherless; maintain the rights
of the poor and oppressed. Rescue the weak and needy; deliver
them from the hand of the wicked." (Psalm 82:3-4 NIV)

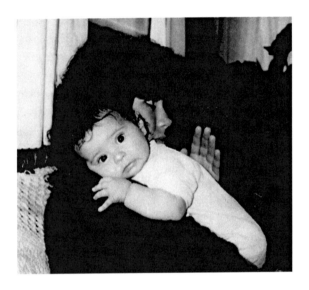

6

Prenatal Violence:

Basics of Fetal Alcohol Spectrum

Author's note: Some of the disabilities common in children, and adopted children, are: Attention Deficit, Hyperactive Disorder (ADHD), Autism/Pervasive Development Disorders, Cerebral Palsy, Cleft Lip & Palate, Cystic Fibrosis, Down Syndrome, Fetal Alcohol Syndrome/Drug Babies, Epilepsy, Hearing Impairment, Learning Disorders, Mental Disorders, Reactive Attachment Disorder (RAD), Speech/Language Disorders, Spina Bifida, etc. Please research these; many books on each exist already.

The following two chapters detail what I consider the "Unexpected Disabilities." I believe these are the problems most often undiagnosed until after adoption or improperly diagnosed as something else. I also believe they're some that present parents with the most frustrating challenges.

The first shot nearly missed; it slid painfully by as it grazed its target. The second came silently but quickly, ripped like buckshot through soft flesh -- leaving a riddled mass behind. Tougher gun control could not have prevented this violence; these shots came from a bottle.

Not long ago, a pregnant woman thought nothing of having a drink to relax. *"Better for the baby if I'm calm instead of stressed,"* she said. Today, the facts are too clear to deny: Alcohol and pregnancy don't mix.

According to the U.S. Department of Health and Human Services, alcohol consumption during pregnancy is the number one cause of mental retardation. Damage varies depending on the amount consumed during pregnancy, but the results are always devastating.

Research from the Centers for Disease Control and Prevention (Ann Streissguthl, 1996) reports the following effects from inutero alcohol exposure:

94% experience mental health problems.

43% have a disrupted school experience (suspension, expulsion or drop out).

60% have trouble with the law.

60% experience confinement (incarceration for crimes or inpatient treatment for mental health, alcohol/drug problems).

30% struggle with drug/alcohol problems and 45% are reported to have inappropriate sexual behaviors.

80% are not capable of living independently when they mature.

Although alarming statistics, the terrifying news is that doctors don't know how much alcohol during pregnancy is too much. In other words, no amount of drinking is safe for a developing infant.

The idea that alcohol permanently damages babies is not a new one. Nevertheless, this knowledge has not spread quickly enough. 1997 studies estimated that one out of every 1000 babies is born alcohol effected. Our economy is burdened by an annual 2.1 billion-dollar expense incurred by these children (and adults).

At least as far back as 1750, letters circulated in English Parliament making these same claims. One such letter referred to the "gin epidemic," "too often the cause of weak, feeble, and distempered children, who must be, instead of an advantage and strength, [become] a charge to their country."

Nineteenth Century, French physician, Dr. E. Lanceraux also described some significant characteristics of Fetal Alcohol Syndrome:

> "As an infant he dies of convulsions or other nervous disorders; if he lives, he becomes idiotic or imbecile, and in adult life bears the special characteristics: the head is small . . ., his physiognomy vacant [peculiar facial features], a nervous susceptibility more or less accentuated, a state of nervousness bordering on hysteria, convulsions, epilepsy... are the sorrowful inheritance,... a great number of individuals given to drink bequeath their children." (Lanceraux, 1865; quoted by Gustafson, 1885).

Nevertheless, issues of prenatal alcohol exposure were ignored then and still are by many today.

During the 1960s, the medical profession condoned moderate alcohol use during pregnancy. Many leading physicians expressed doubt that any relationship between birth defects and alcohol existed.

Today, through breakthroughs in technology, the existence of Fetal Alcohol Syndrome is indisputable. Completely acknowledged now, we know it as "FAS," or in its milder form, Fetal Alcohol Effects, "FAE."

Technology has gone so far as to expose why and how FAS children suffer. X-rays of a healthy infant's brain and one of an FAS effected infant are dramatically different. The FAS child's brain is small and shrunken and lacks an intact corpus callosum, the middle section -- which processes information between the right brain and left brain. It is discernible that this brain has sustained damage to other areas as well:

The Cerebellum: which affects motor control.

The Basal Ganglia: impairing the processing of memory.

The Hippocampus: suppressing learning and memory.

Frontal Lobes: which are vital to impulse control.

The workings of an FAE or FAS person's brain are vastly different from a healthy one. According to studies done by Dr. Edward Riley in San Diego, teachers and parents of these affected children are correct: *FAS/FAE children cannot "act their age."*

Dr. Riley says, "Children with FAS appear to plateau in social abilities at about the 4- to 6-year old level, which suggests arrested development. This interpretation is further supported by Streissguth et al., who found that adolescents and adults with FAS had social abilities age-appropriate for a 6-year old child, and by Steinhausen, et al., who showed that children with the social abilities of FAS did not improve with age."

Even if their IQ is normal, FAS individuals just never seem to get it together. As children, they want to do right, but seldom can. As teenagers and adults, they cannot see cause and effect. Controlling their impulses may seem an impossible task -- even speaking the truth is a challenge. They often say whatever comes to mind, unaware that they are lying.

People with bad character prey on FAS individuals because they are so easily influenced and exploited. Seldom are they the masterminds of a crime, but *they are usually the ones who get caught.*

To many of us, FAS/FAE individuals are more than just statistics. They are our loved ones -- an adopted baby who throws unbelievable tantrums, an adored child who keeps following the wrong crowds, or a relative whose mistakes are bigger than other people's. They are our beloved family members no matter how many times they break our hearts.

As much as we would love to, we cannot erase the damage that's been done. So, for their sakes, we look toward the future. We can protect the children who will be born.

Some day, those future children will become the world's adults. They'll live and love, and they'll write books about us -- about our times, our society, and about FAS. They'll recognize that we knew enough to prevent Fetal Alcohol Syndrome. They'll say that all we needed to do was to spread that knowledge and to hold each other accountable. What they conclude then will depend on what we do today.

Will we promote awareness of the dangers of drinking while pregnant? Will we protect unborn children by monitoring pregnant women who are at risk? Will we end this tragic form of child abuse? You decide.

WHAT ABOUT DRUG BABIES?

It won't hurt you to do some research on the negative effects that prenatal exposure to specific drugs have on children. Despite the media frenzy over "drug babies" (which is now waning in light of the truth), alcohol is proven to be *far more* damaging to an unborn infant than most drugs commonly used by pregnant women.

Drugs are bad, mmkay? Remember, however, expectant mothers who use drugs also usually drink alcohol while pregnant. As a group, "drug using mothers" drink alcohol, use more than one drug, have inadequate nutrition, suffer poor health themselves, and live in polluted environments filled with violence. Drugs or no drugs, these babies are likely to have problems. Although alcohol, (readily available, widely consumed) is *proven* to cause specific and serious birth defects, common drugs such as cocaine are not proven to produce any pattern of serious defects.

Why haven't you heard this? Alcohol is legal, and the alcohol industry is extremely lucrative.

The effects of alcohol on a fetus are far reaching and last a lifetime. Fetal alcohol effects are *often misdiagnosed.* They mimic abandonment issues, post-traumatic stress, attachment disorders, bi-polar, autism, and ADD/ADHD, etc.

If you're adopting, the chances of your baby having fetal alcohol effects depend upon the country of his/her birth. The World Health Organization offers alcohol abuse statistics by country.

This page even has a color-coded map:

http://www.who.int/substance_abuse/facts/alcohol/en/index.html.

For more detailed statistics, country by country, I recommend purchasing the *"Global Status Report on Alcohol 2004"* from the World Health Organization Press or downloading it in .pdf format from their website.

To learn much more about Fetal Alcohol Spectrum, I recommend this website as a starting point:

http://www.come-over.to/FAS/

Last, the *Center for the Evaluation of Risks to Human Reproduction* (CERHR) maintains a comprehensive database of the latest information about potentially hazardous effects of chemicals on human reproduction and development. You can utilize their website to study the various effects of drugs on babies.

7

Nature, Nurture and Nightmares

"... they realized they were naked; so they sewed fig leaves together and made coverings for themselves. Then the man and his wife heard the sound of the LORD God as he was walking in the garden in the cool of the day, and they hid from the LORD God among the trees of the garden.

"But the LORD God called to the man, 'Where are you?' He answered, 'I heard you in the garden, and I was afraid because I was naked; so I hid.'

"And he said, 'Who told you that you were naked? Have you eaten from the tree that I commanded you not to eat from?'" (Genesis 3:7b, 8-11 NIV)

Have you ever done something God *commanded you not to do?* Have you ever been dreaming and suddenly realized you were naked?

Did you think this was mere coincidence?

I have a homework assignment for you: Ask your friends and relatives if they've had this same dream. Be careful who you ask, of course. If you walk up to a stranger and say, *"Have you ever dreamed you were naked?"* it could cause problems. I'm curious about what you'll learn. In all my askings, 100% of the people claim they've had this same dream. You know how it goes: You realize you're naked, you panic and spend the rest of the dream trying to get back home to get dressed, or otherwise trying to find something to cover yourself. In my dreams, I never reached home; never found a covering.

We know that *all have sinned*. Likewise, at some point we all realize we're naked; we try to cover ourselves and hide from God.

Next, I asked born-again Christians (whose lives reflect *Christ*), *"When was the last time you had this dream?"* So far every believer remembers having the dream only *before* they surrendered their lives to Christ; *before* they were clothed with Jesus' righteousness.

> [Jesus speaking] "You say, 'I am rich; I have acquired wealth and do not need a thing.' But you do not realize that you are wretched, pitiful, poor, blind and naked.
> "I counsel you to buy from me gold refined in the fire, so you can become rich; and white clothes to wear, so you can cover your shameful nakedness; and salve to put on your eyes, so you can see.
> Those whom I love I rebuke and discipline. So be earnest, and repent." (Revelation 3:17-19 NIV)

If I ever meet a born-again believer who keeps dreaming they're exposed and panicked about it, I'll be a little confused and very concerned for them.

In the world of psychology, intelligent people often spend their lives seeking answers (in the most complicated ways) to the simplest questions. If they refuse to accept God's words, they must take the long way around to finding the facts. Such was the long and bumpy road to discovery of how a child develops emotionally, mentally, and in respect to his talents or inclinations, etc. At last, the argument over *nature verses nurture* has quieted. The truth that *both* impact the child is almost unanimously accepted now. *"Nativism"* is currently up for discussion. In the field of psychology, *nativism* is the view that certain skills or abilities are "native" or "hard-wired" into the brain at birth.

People can save themselves a lot of time and energy if they'll believe the Bible; as you read through history as recorded in the scripture, you see that God creates each of us with certain talents and purposes.

> "For we are God's workmanship, created in Christ Jesus to do good works, which God prepared in advance for us to do." (Ephesians 2:10 NIV)

Since both nature and nurture are instrumental in a child's development, many people wonder, when a person exhibits neurotic behaviors, is that because of defective genes or is this the result of a dysfunctional childhood? They wrongly assume that the natural state of man, without any negative influence or defective genetic material, is an ideal person. In the beginning -- in the Garden of Eden -- this was probably true.

We're not in the Garden anymore.

Return to our discussion in *Chapter Three*: Aside from any good effects from nurturing or any negative from abuse and neglect, what *is* the natural state of a person at birth? prior to a spiritual rebirth? All people are slaves to their fallen or sin nature. Any "likeness of God" (as we were created in God's likeness) is overshadowed and corrupted by the fallen nature. We're naked; sewing leaves together, and trying to hide from God.

> "So I say, live by the Spirit, and you will not gratify the desires of the sinful nature. For the sinful nature desires what is contrary to the Spirit, and the Spirit what is contrary to the sinful nature. They are in conflict with each other, so that you do not do what you want. But if you are led by the Spirit, you are not under law.
>
> "The acts of the sinful nature are obvious: sexual immorality, impurity and debauchery; idolatry and witchcraft; hatred, discord, jealousy, fits of rage, selfish ambition, dissensions, factions and envy; drunkenness, orgies, and the like. I warn you, as I did before, that those who live like this will not inherit the kingdom of God.
>
> "But the fruit of the Spirit is love, joy, peace, patience, kindness, goodness, faithfulness, gentleness and self-control. Against such things there is no law. Those who belong to Christ Jesus have crucified the sinful nature with its passions and desires. Since we live by the Spirit, let us keep in step with the Spirit. Let us not become conceited, provoking and envying each other." (Galatians 5:16-26 NIV)

The acts of the sinful nature are... sinful. We know from scripture (and life experience) that engaging in and practicing sinful behavior has a devastating and destructive effect on a person's mental and emotional state. Neuroticism and other negative traits are enhanced and encouraged through our exposure and surrender to sinful behavior and urges.

All people are hard-wired with two opposite *potentials:* If living *by the Spirit of God,* His beauty and goodness *can* flow from their lives. If living ruled by their sinful nature, horrible and hurtful things will dominate their minds, rot their emotions, and exhibit through their actions.

In light of the opposite potentials that war within each person, what part does nurture play?

Never having experienced spiritual rebirth or life *by the Spirit of God*, children are born carnal; they're merely physical beings, *led by their natural desires* and *conforming to social influences* around them. They're spiritually asleep, stuck in *Romans, Chapter 7...* waiting for Chapter Eight.

In this realm the effects of nurture (or neglect) are *profound.*

KINGS AND MONKEYS

In the 13th Century AD, Frederick II, King of Germany, conducted an experiment to determine what language a child would speak if he/she were not spoken to in infancy or the early years.

The King placed a number of babies with foster mothers or nurses. He gave strict orders that no one speak to or play with the babies. His orders were followed, but his experiment failed.

All of the babies died due to a lack of attention.

Later, the Mogul Emperor Akbar tried to determine what religion children would adopt if raised in isolation. His experiment also failed.

All of the children turned out deaf and mute.

To those who know God's nature, these experiments are not only vile, but also absurd; even a monkey could have told them they'd fail. In the end, it *was* a monkey -- or a group of monkeys -- who gave the hard-hearted world "scientific proof" that babies need love.

During the 1950s and 60s, an American psychologist named Harry Frederick Harlow caused quite a stir with his maternal-separation and social isolation experiments on Rhesus monkeys. Despite serious ethical concerns regarding the cruel experiments, he did demonstrate the importance of tangible affection in social and cognitive development of baby monkeys.

In Mr. Harlow's beginning research, his interest was sparked when the baby monkeys didn't respond as expected. Taken from their mothers within hours of birth, they received milk from a bottle attached to the cage. Rather than becoming attached to the bottle or nipple (the source of the life-giving milk), they were fixated on the soft cloth diapers that lined the bottom of their cages. They seemed comforted not by the milk, but by cuddling with the soft cloth; this strange bond baffled the scientist and he began further experiments into the phenomenon.

He next presented the monkeys with two surrogate "mothers"; some monkeys had both and some had one or the other. Both "mothers" had a face with eyes; one was made entirely of wire and the other was covered with soft terry cloth material. Sometimes the babies received milk through a hole in the wire "mother," and sometimes through the cloth "mother." Regardless, the baby monkeys clung to the soft terry-cloth mother for comfort and security, whether that mother gave them milk or not. The baby monkeys who were raised with either a wire mother or a cloth mother gained weight at the same rate. However, the monkeys that had *only a wire mother* had trouble digesting the milk and suffered from diarrhea more often.

Whenever a frightening stimulus was brought into the cage, the monkeys ran to the cloth mother for protection and comfort, no matter which mother provided them with food; this response decreased as the monkeys grew older.

When the monkeys were placed in an unfamiliar room with their cloth mother, they clung to it until they felt secure enough to explore. Once they began to explore, they occasionally returned to the cloth mother for comfort. Monkeys placed in an unfamiliar room *without* their cloth mothers acted quite differently; they froze in fear and cried, crouched down, or sucked their thumbs. Some monkeys even ran from object to object, apparently searching for the cloth mother, as they cried and screamed. Monkeys placed in this situation with their wire mothers exhibited the same behavior as the monkeys with no mother; without the soft mother to run to, they could not cope but would scream, run in circles, and urinate.

If you spend enough time working with abused children, at some point you'll feel like you've stumbled into Harlow's lab.

Yes, it gets worse. Harlow next did isolation experiments on the baby monkeys. Partial isolation resulted in various abnormalities such as blank staring, repetitive circling in their cages, and self-mutilation. Total isolation experiments produced monkeys that were severely psychologically disturbed.

The damage was permanent; he was never able to successfully integrate them into society.

Since these experiments, much more research followed regarding nurturing and development of human children. Although the full truth will never be found in psychology because of its many false assumptions and reprehensible methods, there is truth in statistics. Studies clearly prove that humans are permanently impacted by their experiences during infancy and the first two years of life. As if naked, wearing leaves and hiding from God weren't bad enough... if abused, neglected, or isolated during this stage, without a miracle, the damage is lasting.

But of course, I believe in miracles.

8

Homemade Glue for Unattached Kids

Lindsay is only three years old, but she knows how to work a party. Within minutes of entering a room full of strangers, she has all eyes on her. She grins and wiggles and waves; she's forgotten her adoptive parents standing in the foyer, astonished, watching her show. When it's time to go home, she kicks and screams; she wants to go home with the nice man who gave her a cookie.

Tyler is five. For him, happiness means staring into a *Disney* movie all day long. He comes back to reality from time to time if he's really hungry. He is an overly sweet and loving child... when he wants something. He usually refuses to be held or hugged, but he'll let a puppy lick his face for hours.

Brittany is six years old, and she's been called "the child from hell" on more than one occasion. I have to draw the line here; this is a cruel and unacceptable thing to say about a child. However, I will admit that the chant "redrum, redrum" (from the movie *The Shining*) does come to mind when watching Brittany scheme or scream.

What do these kids have in common? Most were born into violence, neglect, or serious instability. Many have never had a place to call home, just multiple pit stops. They're charming beyond words, even overly affectionate at times, but only on their terms. They're miniature control-freaks; masters of manipulation.

Often, they've been diagnosed with "Reactive Attachment Disorder." They can spot a soft touch a mile off, and they don't understand the concept of returning genuine love.

Therapists and caseworkers meet daily, struggling with the issues these un-bonded children cause.

"Where can we put her now? I was hoping she wouldn't get herself kicked out of this home!" How much counseling will they need before they make the list of "adoptable" children? If they're adopted, will it last?

Some sit in shelters for years because they're just not ready to meet the world; or rather, the world is not prepared to meet them. It's an understatement to say these children are difficult to parent.

Some of us are relatives (grandparents, aunts, or uncles, etc.), or foster or adoptive parents who have stepped in to fill a parent's empty shoes. We love these kids, despite the all-day violent screaming fits, constant testing of boundaries, lying, stealing, and bizarre behaviors.

So while the therapists, counselors, and caseworkers juggle their caseloads of children like ours, we must find a way to make things work. Support and resources are valuable, but no one knows or loves these children as we do, and the game is played at home.

What can you do? Start with an old-fashioned recipe for spoiled kids.

These children haven't had the love they needed nor the stability, but most of them have a serious case of the "gimees." Some are in "survival" mode; they've been forced to fight to get their needs met. They see human relationships only as a means of getting something. They've never felt safe, secure, and cherished, so they seek a peaceful feeling by controlling everything and everyone around them.

Others, especially American children who've been in foster-care, have been more or less, raised by strangers. How does a stranger try to earn the trust of a child? Gifts!

Caseworkers bring teddy bears and coloring books. Therapists hand out flashy little trinkets and each new foster parent tries to make friends with them by saying, "Look, Honey, this is for you!" Many have had cookies and toys and movies and new clothing from the government every six months. They expect that adults are bearing gifts, and they've rarely -- or never -- experienced a relationship that went beyond receiving things; for this reason, forget for a moment that these children are scared and emotionally wounded. Start by addressing their "control-freak tendencies," or their "spoiled brat syndrome."

FIRST STEP:

No. The answer is no. She'll kick and scream and throw things. She'll hate you. She'll want to go home with the man who drives her to visitations. She'll demand things she doesn't even want just to be in control.

The gentle, firm answer must be no. No new toys, no goodies, no rides on the carousel horse. No one (not teachers, strangers, or even Grandma) may be allowed to give her gifts.

This is a difficult step, but the issue is control. You must help this child to forget the quest for control by allowing nothing that she demands. Remind your child that "all she needs (besides food, clothing and shelter) is love." It takes patience, but sooner or later she'll learn to see and want YOU, rather than what you can give her.

SECOND STEP:

I'm your only hope, kid. Believe it or not, a baby learns to love his parents out of necessity. He looks up one day and says to himself, "Wow! If you weren't here, I'd be all alone. If you didn't feed me, I'd go hungry... I think I'm in love!"

Your un-bonded child has never traveled this path. Those he looked to either continually left him and were replaced by someone else, or they allowed him to suffer with his basic needs unmet. It's your job to take him through a positive, natural parental-nurturing experience.

Two basic rules will set the train in motion:

DON'T TALK TO STRANGERS: It's so important that your child learn to deal with the world through you. You're his avenue to everything! Egotistical as it may sound, it's the essence of security for a young child; it's the beginning of his healing.

ALWAYS ASK MOM OR DAD: He must not be allowed to control or manipulate people – this will reinforce his feeling that he's alone against the world. You must be the key to everything he wants or needs. He can't ask anyone else for permission; no, not even Grandma. Your child needs to need you and learn to trust your judgment. Likewise, he can't be allowed to make decisions for himself now if he is to grow to be a healthy adult. If he learns to love and trust you, then he may begin to make wise choices because his desires will stem from more healthful motivating factors.

Don't worry if the storm gets worse before it gets better. A *new way of relating to people* will only be learned if the other, more familiar path is blocked off.

How strictly and for how long will you need to follow this plan? Every child is different. Keep a diary and consult it often. Begin to give more freedom when you see results, but less if you see that progress is being lost.

I recently sat in on a discussion with many home schooling parents who had moved to the country in search of a simpler way of life. They quickly realized rural living provides fewer opportunities for their children to socialize outside of the family unit.

After moving, they noticed something truly amazing and shocking happening to their children. Suddenly, these siblings began to enjoy each other's company! Where they had previously considered each other nuisances, they now were cherished friends... because there was no one else to play with!

God, in His ultimate wisdom and mercy, created the human emotions to be predictable. Guard and channel your child's precious emotions. Pray for direction as you teach your child to love and trust. Some children will respond quickly. If he or she were severely damaged from lack of nurture as an infant and toddler, you may see only slow improvement. Persevere. Pray without ceasing until your child receives the miracle healing that only God can give.

> "For you created my inmost being; you knit me together in my mother's womb. I praise you because I am fearfully and wonderfully made; your works are wonderful, I know that full well." (Psalm 139: 13-14 NIV)

Part Three:
War Stories

INTRODUCTION to Part Three

Congratulations, you've reached the final part of the book! I hope you're feeling more prepared; I apologize if you're now terrified at the prospect of adopting or doing fostercare. However, it gives me great hope to see you here, still reading.

Maybe you're scared, excited, or both. Maybe you've decided to enlist, or you're pretty sure you've been drafted. In any event, you're here with me now and I suspect you'll probably get orders soon. Now, before you go, you've earned the right to come in to the circle, sit down, and listen as we swap war stories . . .

The following true stories are written by me or by parents who've volunteered to share their adoption experiences with you because they care. We've all heard touching stories of successful, *easy* adoptions; many have experienced those, *praise God!* Rarely do you hear about the other side of adoption. Many of us have those stories as well, but we usually keep quiet about them; we're too sad, frustrated, discouraged, or ashamed to talk about the difficulties and heartbreak. I understand, but remember, there's freedom in honesty and truth. Potential adoptive parents have a right to the *whole* story.

The families who've participated in this section have mild stories compared with many that I know. I wish the other parents could share, but they're not ready; they entered adoption as close-knit, happy families – some already had well-adjusted biological children. These parents were excited, perhaps idealistically so, and were going to save a child! Now, many are divorced, their biological children have been abused and molested, and in some cases, even taken away from them because their homes became unsafe.

Many went into adoption completely unprepared, and we've struggled and learned everything the hard way. On one hand, it's uplifting for me to hear that I'm not the only one who doesn't breeze through my days as an adoptive mommy; on the other hand, it breaks my heart that so many parents experienced extreme frustration, confusion, and heartache.

We could have been spared seasons of believing we were failures if only we'd known *what was going on*. Many of us were already experienced, *good* parents, so we couldn't understand why all of our parenting methods failed with these children.

My experiences will be different from yours because I didn't have any of the information that you've already read in this book! My adoptions are also different from many other moms, because I didn't set out intending to adopt; in fact, it was the opposite.

We already had three biological children, so I purposely became licensed for "temporary shelter" fostercare only. We didn't want the risk of getting attached. Yet, even though I was only supposed to foster children for a few days to a month, the fostercare system in my city became overloaded. Some of these *temporary placements* lasted a year or a year-and-a-half; their cases progressed to severance, and they needed an adoptive family. By that time, they were already part of our family; so we adopted... three times!

I've helped other moms to go into fostercare specifically looking to adopt. I tell them to become licensed for "regular fostercare" or "fost-adopt/legal risk" if they want infants -- you are the boss and you choose the ages you'll take. It's reasonable to say that you'll care for babies under one year old only. The amount of placements you receive and whether or not they're substance-affected really depends on your location. If you're in an area with a large population, there will be more babies coming into fostercare; if you live way out in the country... well, maybe none.

Also, if you live in a community with a high incidence of substance abuse, then you can expect that more of the infants coming into care will have issues from being substance exposed.

One thing I'm repeatedly asked by hopeful parents is this: Is there a risk that I'll care for a child and then have to give him/her back? The answer is yes.

There's always a risk that you'll love a child that you don't keep. Even domestic or international adoption can go awry and break hearts... even biological children can leave us long before we want them to. My oldest biological daughter was diagnosed with an inoperable, cancerous brain tumor at age two; she lived just six more months after her diagnosis. Any type of parenting makes you vulnerable to heartbreak.

If you do fostercare long enough, you'll usually end up adopting. If you're a "regular foster" parent, you usually care for a few that go home before one sticks. The instance of this is lower in "fost-adopt" placements – please see the Glossary for clarification.

Not every parent is okay with this, but I viewed the temporary children as a type of babysitting. I enjoyed them while I had them, pray for them still, and hope I added something positive to their lives.

As for the ones we adopted, while they were in the "limbo" stage, my goal was to let them live their lives without a care in the world, so I bore the stress of limbo-status for them. They were too young to understand the uncertainty of their future, so why worry them? Childhood is short and I wanted theirs to be as happy and normal as possible.

As I mentioned, my adoptions have not been easy, but remember I was not looking to adopt. If I had been, and knew the things I know now, then my experiences raising adopted children would probably be easier. I adopted difficult kids. They came into our family separately – but all had experienced pain, fear, neglect, and extreme inconsistency from the adults in their lives. They'd never experienced any sort of bonding, and they're also fetal-alcohol and drug exposed; one developed autism as well. Of course, most issues were undetected until after we'd begun raising them; hence, my confusion. Many times after adoption, I shook my head and thought, what in the world is wrong with *me*? I used to be a good mother, now I'm a horrible failure.

Looking back now, it all makes sense; however, in the beginning I didn't know where all the disturbing behaviors were coming from. These children were "perfectly healthy"... *on the outside*. It was only later we discovered the fetal-alcohol effects were causing issues, and they were also evaluated and "labeled" as children who have no capacity to bond (however, I have seen miracles).

I had many moments where I figured God couldn't possibly have wanted them with me... I felt I was doing a pitiful job raising them... but eventually I always returned to this thought:

If I were a child - helpless, homeless, without family or love - and I had the choice of being without a family forever or having Cheryl (pitiful as she is) as my mommy... what would I choose?

So we survived and continued on, but I still struggled with guilt because I didn't feel as strong of a bond with some as I thought I should. In my mind, I was passionate about being a loving mother, but my emotions felt... anemic. I was so tired. Many times I prayed, asking for forgiveness for my feelings of apathy and for help to feel a deep parental love for these kids; still it was lacking.

One day, I realized something vital: The only love that was missing was the "natural" love - the feeling of a bond between mother and child. Under natural circumstances, this strong emotional bond motivates and guides the parents as they protect and raise their child. However, adoption *isn't natural* and these children are not as they should have been (without damage); they have extra challenges and I've been called to have something higher than natural love.

> "If you love those who love you, what reward will you get? Are not even the tax collectors doing that? And if you greet only your brothers, what are you doing more than others? Do not even pagans do that?" (Matthew 5:46-47 NIV)

My lack of strong emotion actually *was the natural response* to this situation!

Not only was it *my* natural response; I've since learned that many adoptive parents of troubled children experience the same condition. If you're raising a child who is a chronic liar, steals anything and everything not nailed down; methodically tears holes in every piece of clothing as soon as you give it to them (and their blankets too); digs holes in the walls near their bed (even in the mattresses); who watches you *constantly* out of the corner of their eye (waiting for you to look away so they can break something, etc.); who victimizes other children and pets; needs 24-hour supervision to keep from making themselves violently ill by eating non-edible items (trash, dog food, shampoo -- whatever); who responds to correction or discipline by urinating (or worse) in their pants; and his or her greatest goal and dream in life is to run away from home...

You might *not* form a strong emotional bond with this child, but that's okay because you can still *love* them; God's love is *supernatural*.

> "Therefore, as God's chosen people, holy and dearly loved, clothe yourselves with compassion, kindness, humility, gentleness and patience. Bear with each other and forgive whatever grievances you may have against one another. Forgive as the Lord forgave you." (Colossians 3:12-13 NIV)

Since I realized the above, my goals became clearer; it's a *mission* – or ministry -- and that's the main point. Yes, I'm *parenting*, but under these circumstances, the typical parental feelings may or may not blossom; it doesn't matter. My mission is to nurture these kids, include them as part of a loving family, teach them scripture, and pray God will touch them in a powerful way and call them into a relationship with Himself. Nothing else matters.

My mission has been hard and will continue to be so – because I'm weak. But God is strong and faithful; He answers prayer, and I still truly and wholeheartedly believe in miracles.

9

The Hospice Survivor
By Cheryl Ellicott

The night was hot and I was cold.

I stood in the dark as the ceiling fan spun above my head and my thoughts turned circles through my mind. *I'm tired and I've earned my rest—I'm four babies past my eighteenth year, and I'd like to sit down before I'm thirty.* Just as fast as I conceived one thought, another came whirling through:

Never grow weary of doing good, for in due season you will reap a harvest... if you do not give up.

Despite my uncertainty that hot summer night, I agreed to take a foster daughter into my home to live with my husband, me, and our four small children. Not just another foster child, but a seventeen-year-old girl with a baby.

Never grow weary of doing good... for in due time you will reap a harvest.

I cradled the late night call in the palm of my hand, hesitating before I responded to the voice on the other end. I stared out the window into the dark Arizona night, remembering nights when I was zealous. When God's love was as real to me as the dark that now embraced the city of Tucson. I recalled days when my faith seemed stronger, but those were hard times; while girls my age fretted over who they'd go to the prom with, I'd kept company with a hospice nurse. I held my own baby girl's hand as the cancer slowly took her from me... only my faith kept my heart from breaking into a million pieces.

Yet, I hadn't felt drained back then. I wondered now if I were drifting toward the death of my closeness with Jesus—beyond the point of caring whether or not I would reap a harvest; sometimes I get tired like that. So tired. Usually it scares me; this time was no exception... that's why I said yes.

"When will you bring them?" I held the phone up to my mouth now. The familiar voice of the CPS worker answered with the usual answer,

"I'm not sure."

"Okay," I said, "I'll be ready," but I wasn't.

My foster daughter's name was Tia. At nearly six feet tall and with a booming alto voice, she was accustomed to getting her own way. Even with her boyfriend—a drug dealer in jail for attempted murder—she was the boss.

She hated healthful food and demanded canned corned-beef-hash and Pepsi. She wanted the bed disassembled so she could throw the mattress on the floor to sleep, like she was used to. She refused to put her baby, Danielle, in the crib or in generic brand diapers!

Also, Tia liked to burn candles at night... thinking they would hide the smell of her marijuana smoke as it drifted through the halls of my home.

Tia was "*all ghetto,*" as she liked to say.

It took me a few crazy, everything-up-in-the-air days before I realized what was happening. My first thought came easily, *You don't need this. Send them on their way.* I was tempted to look the other way, wait until she turned eighteen or just have her moved to a shelter; let someone else worry about her. The second thought was harder... but I knew what God wanted.

Never grow weary of doing good... do not give up.

I knew that I had to stand up tall, no matter how tired I was, and look this big girl in the eyes and act like a real mother to her. Maybe I wasn't feeling super zealous these days, but Tia needed love strong enough to tell her what to do... if not just for herself, for the sake of baby Danielle.

Standing beneath the thumping, rattling loose ceiling fan, I wondered if I could do what was best. *Lord? I'm not strong enough. She's too intense, too determined, too angry – too big! Surely you wouldn't expect me to bridle a bull. Did I forget to tell you how exhausted I am?*

I held my weary head within my small hands and sighed long and deep. I stayed there, praying, for longer than I'd prayed in a long, long time. My only other choice was to send her on her way... I could see only these two ways to go.

In due time you will reap a harvest, if you do not give up.

So I gathered up my small, thin self and marched off to bridle the bull.

I never did control her, but she opened her heart to me; that was something. Suddenly, all her anger and hurt came gushing out like a torrential flood seeking to drown everything in its way.

Tia's mama had died from cancer; it was generally accepted that Mom's drug use caused the cancer. Tia sat beside me night after endless night and praised the virtue of her mother, but I saw the anger just beneath her words. Maybe it was Mom's fault that Tia was abused by the flow of damaged people floating through their lives. It probably was wrong that Mom allowed Tia to smoke marijuana to calm her frayed nerves. However, during those last days, after Tia had been nursing her dying mother for nine months, didn't Mom make everything right? Didn't she apologize for not being there when Tia needed her?

How could you be angry with someone when you had changed their diapers and held their trembling hand when the cancer stole them away? Tia couldn't, but she could be angry with her foster mother. She could test her foster mom's love and expect that love to be strong enough to erase any neglect her own mother had shown her.

Meanwhile, I could sit beneath my whining, squeaking ceiling fan, (which badly needed oiling) praying again, praying harder than I had since my own daughter was stricken with cancer, so many years ago. I wondered how I could possibly deal with Tia; I knew I couldn't heal her pain.

Lord? I don't swim well enough to carry the weight of two! Oh sure, you've carried me through my valleys—even the shadow of death—but what do I know? Surely this broken child will pull us both under and we'll drown! She, scrambling and gasping for air; me, killing myself in an effort to hold her up! Or... maybe I'll be lucky and just be smothered to death...

Still the same answer came back to me:

Do not give up.

So, even though I felt guilty for my lack of fervor, I kept going.

At the end of two months, I sat with the phone between clenched fists. I'd had enough. Sure, she was reading the Bible by then, asking questions, confessing hope in Jesus Christ to set her free from the crazy mixed-up emotions that tossed her about. Yet...

Tia was still an enormous brat; I was losing my patience and seeing a side of myself I didn't like.

"You need to tell me what Jesus says about this!" "I don't wanna read for myself!" "You only love your kids, you don't love me!" Tia would whine day after day, night after night. "Why do you cook this stuff?" "Why do you wear your hair like that?" "I couldn't follow that rule because..."

Again and again, she had emergencies at curfew time and couldn't make it home.

She was assaulted twice in two weeks; she totaled her car; and five times, she went to the emergency room. She fought against everything I asked her to do. Oh sure, later she'd come back and tell me she was sorry. "I love you and you were right."

But honestly, Tia was driving me crazy.

So that day came and I was sitting there feeling sick to my stomach, holding the phone and dialing the number to have Tia and her baby moved to separate shelters; there were no shelters that would take both a teenage girl and her baby.

Why? Why are you giving up?

I answered,

What can I do for such a rebellious girl? Nothing I say helps her—she's in my face all day long! She's bigger than me, louder than me... and why do I wear my hair like this anyway?

I wanted to scream, but held back.

Oh, I know she's wrong but what can I do? I can't handle this disobedient girl.

Then the phone line was busy, so I picked up my Bible to pass the time.

My bookmark lay inside the book of Matthew, in Chapter 21. I read the parable of the two sons, replaced the bookmark, and dialed the number again. When it began to ring I set the receiver back into its cradle.

"*Which of the two sons did what his father wanted?*" Jesus asked. The people answered, "*It was the first son.*"

My mind replayed the story as I sat and listened, knowing what it meant; it wasn't the agreeable son, in the end, who did what his father wanted. The truly obedient son first said to his father, "*No! I will not,*" but later he changed his mind and went. Suddenly, I saw things as they really were.

Which child is Tia? He asked.

She's the first child, Lord. The one who says, "I will not!" and then later changes her mind and does what she should.

I smiled, pushed the phone away and the sick feeling in my stomach resided.

She's the obedient one.

With that realization came the shocking truth that Tia was sent to help me, not the other way around. Yet, she hadn't come to watch me die because I wasn't really terminal. I could see now that I'd never been more full of zeal, faith, and the power of God. No, I'd just been in circumstances that brought me shaking and crying into His strong arms.

Maybe God had been missing me lately... so He'd brought me Tia. So I kept her for awhile longer, though I couldn't change her.

I spent many more days and nights leading her through scriptures to find the answers she needed and praying that God would comfort her in her grief and heal her broken heart. Yet even the Apostle Paul, each time he preached in a city, would eventually realize it was time to move on. In my case, there were no big rocks or death-threats involved, but when I felt my marriage and my relationship with my other children were about to crumble, I had Tia and baby Danielle moved.

After they'd gone, I lay down, watching that silly fan sit there and do nothing on a cold night, and I was warm. I prayed and the presence of God surrounded me like a living blanket. I knew things had never been just about me or about how much I had to give.

No, God's plans were always much bigger than that.

It's been ten years since I first met Tia. She's in her late twenties now and for a long time it looked like she'd just keep traveling the same path her biological mom took her down. I stood by helpless, watching her become the mother of two baby girls, then three... then four. Different fathers, never a husband. She moved far away and eventually stopped calling and writing altogether. I didn't hear from her for years and I wondered, *did I fail?* Were my efforts in vain? Had my prayers come to nothing? I realized that no, even then, it was obvious something amazing had happened. My spiritual cancer was still in remission; God did a work in *my heart,* through Tia.

Also, I knew my prayers for Tia and her children were still there; permanently etched in the fabric of the unseen... they would be answered in God's perfect timing.

Then one day, just before the final edit and publishing of this story, Tia found me again; a calmer, happier Tia, no longer the wild young woman, restless and troubled. She's now happily married, almost ready to graduate from college... and she still calls me Mom.

> "... a man reaps what he sows... the one who sows to please the Spirit, from the Spirit will reap eternal life. Let us not become weary in doing good, for at the proper time we will reap a harvest if we do not give up . . ." (Galatians 6:8-9 NIV)

I'm surrounded by miracles.

10

My Adoption Kinship Story
By Malee Razzaia

I clearly remember the day our journey into adoption began. A phone number appeared on my cell phone that I hadn't seen for a long while; it was a call from my sweet May -- a big eyed, pouty lipped, beautiful little girl who God had now transformed into a woman. How time flew by.

This dear, young lady always had a special place in my heart. We met when she was only eight years old. She was timid and shy, but we took to each other right away. Her mother met my husband Paul through work and we through them. We had two things in common: we each had a parent from Taiwan and we shared the same nickname.

May didn't know her Taiwanese father, so I helped her connect with her Asian heritage. I taught her to cook, speak Taiwanese, and eventually she learned how to care for my own children who were a wee one and two years old at the time.

Through her childhood, May and I remained close. She'd call anytime she needed something or someone with whom to talk. I felt like an aunt to her. May was at our home often.

Eventually, May's visits became less and less as she changed from the sweet little May-May we'd known into an isolated and rebellious young woman. We prayed for her and tried reaching out to her. She used to enjoy attending church with us, but now she declined. We continued to pray for May, but after high school we almost never heard from her.

Suddenly one day, after a long silence, she called.

"I'm pregnant," she said in the middle of our catch-up conversation. She started crying as she went on to tell me that her Mom had suggested an abortion. I encouraged her to have the baby.

"We'll get through it May-May. I'll help you," I said. God had brought May back into my life and I was excited to have another chance to try and reach her with the hope I knew she needed.

On a cool winter day in February, May's baby Keillani was born. I loved this beautiful baby the minute I saw her. During pregnancy, May seemed happy about the baby. After Keillani was born, May welcomed nursing her, but only for a short time.

When May stopped nursing, I told myself not to worry; not all mommies nurse... but when May didn't buy any formula, I couldn't help worrying. Although May and her baby needed assistance badly, she didn't sign up for the programs that were readily available. She also failed to make the routine doctor's appointments for Keillani. People around her were scraping to provide for the baby, and trying to encourage May to be responsible. She had excuses for each thing that wasn't done, but they didn't make sense. None of it made sense to me... at the time.

When Keillani was two weeks old, May decided to begin working. I gladly volunteered to baby sit. After all, who could pass up the opportunity to spend time with a precious newborn and share the hope of the gospel with an unsaved Mommy as well? I was going to be that *Titus 2* older woman, mentoring this young mother – or so I thought.

May's days at work grew longer and longer. Soon, Baby Keillani began staying with me even when May was not at work; May claimed she needed to do errands. I decided we needed boundaries when May asked me if I could keep Keillani while she and her friends took a vacation to Cancun. I explained to her that, as a Mommy, she needed to include the baby in her day as much as possible. I was encouraged because she seemed to understand and agree. Things were looking up.

The next day, she called me from work sobbing. "I need to talk to you right away," she said. "Can I come see you right now?" I agreed, but didn't have the slightest idea why she was so upset and needed to come see me right away, nor did I realize that my life was about to be forever changed.

When May arrived, I was shocked by her words: "I want to give Keillani up for adoption," she said between tears. "I want you and Paul to adopt Keillani." She went on to explain open adoption to me. She said she was not ready to parent. She didn't want Keillani raised by a single Mom and she wanted to go back to school. I was speechless. I'd never imagined she was contemplating this.

I then started down the road with my many mistakes in the adoption process.

"You don't really mean this." I said. "You just need some time to think about it. I know things must be stressful." On and on I went, trying to convince May that she really wanted to parent. I minimized her feelings and assumed she wasn't serious. I convinced myself, and May as well, that she just had post-partum depression; it was temporary and soon she'd feel like parenting.

Eventually, I talked her out of adoption and into giving my family temporary legal guardianship. May would remain the Mommy and we would care for the baby while she adjusted to her role as parent.

At first May visited daily. She took the baby on outings to show her friends. She'd call on days when she couldn't come over. She seemed responsible, and I was hopeful it would turn into real parenting soon.

However, when time went by and post-partum should have waned, and when May never went back to school as she'd said she would, I was confused. When things did not progress, it finally hit me. My sweet May was content leaving things as they were. She enjoyed the relationship with her baby but never intended on taking responsibility. She'd been telling me that from the start, when she asked us to adopt. She said she wasn't ready to parent and didn't want to; I assumed she didn't know what she really wanted.

I couldn't imagine not wanting to parent this baby! The feelings of responsibility toward Keillani came so naturally for me. Now I believe it came natural because God was preparing me; He knew this little one was soon to become my daughter.

As time passed, Keillani was more and more tearful after each visit with May. She missed her mother and didn't understand the long leaves of absence. Their bond was being maintained, but Keillani's heart was broken over and over again each time May walked out the door. I tried to soothe her cries but was becoming discouraged; I was bonding deeply with this sweet baby – and she was missing her mommy.

Eventually, with the help of godly counsel, I realized it was time to set real boundaries. There could be only one mommy – as God had created it. Keillani was confused and hurting. May would have to make the choice all over again. Would she take on the full role of Mother, or would I? Either way, we could not make Keillani live in limbo any longer.

Deep inside, I was hoping May would choose to parent Keillani, and she did. We agreed to start a transition plan to place Keillani completely in May's care within two months. I offered to remain available for support. My heart was both broken and relieved. Broken for me, yet relieved that Keillani was still little enough to adjust well.

The next day, however, May changed her mind again. She said she really did not want to parent. She returned to her original plan and asked us to adopt. Only this time, it wasn't as easy for her. By prolonging the adoption process, May had become reattached to Keillani – but not enough to accept the responsibilities of parenting: With more heartstrings tied, the bond would not be transferred as easily this time. I could see May's heart was broken and she was also angry that we had insisted upon an all-or-nothing placement with Keillani. May wanted to continue the guardianship indefinitely – keeping her relationship while we took all of the responsibility. We learned that by minimizing May's initial feelings, we had prolonged both her and Keillani's grief process.

With the adoption papers signed and the home study process beginning, our second mistake was to allow frequent, fully open adoption visits.

May asked for weekly visits and we agreed readily; after all, I reasoned that she was the one losing and I was gaining. I didn't want to add to May's grief. I still didn't understand that I was protecting May's feelings at the cost of Keillani's.

Eventually, May's visits were sporadic and we reduced the visits to once a month. Of course May resisted, as she did each time; however, we realized we must claim more rights to protect Keillani.

Keillani was almost two years old by the time the adoption finalized. The visits were still monthly. Because May's visits were still this frequent, Keillani maintained a bond with her. Adoption day was a tough one as May wanted to be present at the courthouse. May tried to be supportive, but she was heartbroken. Keillani sensed her grief and clung to May after the court proceeding. When it was time to leave, we had to pull her away from her mother as she cried and sobbed along with May.

It was not the most positive adoption picture.

Visits are now quarterly. Keillani has been able to finally attach and bond with us, her forever family. May is seen as a special extended aunt now.

It just breaks my heart that I didn't have the courage to embrace and entitle myself to Keillani sooner. I made the mistake of putting May's feelings over Keillani's welfare; the baby should have come first but instead, we extended and increased her grieving process. Now, there are bitter feelings and broken hearts on all sides. I pray other adoptive families (and birthparents) will learn from my mistakes!

> Don't make promises to a birthparent unless it has the *child's best interests* at heart.

> Put the *needs of the child first* – above the pity you may feel for the birthparents.

Keillani is doing much better today, but I wish I had protected her heart sooner.

11

Supermom Meets Fetal Alcohol
By Emily LeChene

When I was asked to share my story as a foster and then adoptive parent for *This Means War*, I thought, *no way!* Words cannot describe what a difficult season this is for me. Share my story? I didn't even want to *think* about my chaotic life, let alone tell the world. To encourage me to share, Cheryl gave me a rough-draft copy of *This Means War*.

Even opening the book terrified me, so I put it aside and didn't read it.

The author knows my experiences more than most. As a close friend, I've shared my frustrations and anxiety with her over the past five years – since I began my journey into fostercare and later adoption. She was there when we were a happy family with five biological children. She was also there after we adopted, as the stress began to break our peaceful, close-knit family to pieces.

When I finally broke down and read *This Means War*, it opened my eyes. I was encouraged and strengthened through the knowledge that I'm not alone. I realized that my story also has the power to help others as they prepare to foster or adopt -- or who may feel alone in the battle -- as I so often have; for these reasons, I've decided to share.

Cheryl and Mike are long time friends of our family. Through the years, Cheryl called me her "home-schooling mentor." I was home schooling for years before most people had even heard of the concept. Before her own babies reached school age, Cheryl determined that she also would home educate her children. Our worlds revolved around loving God and family, home schooling our children, and the tight budget that so often comes with the decision to be a stay-at-home mom; it was great to have a friend with whom I shared so much in common.

The role of mentor has now been reversed as Cheryl has been there to guide me through the process of fostering and then adoption. She is a woman who hangs on and trusts God through the impossible. She's given me courage to go on when I knew I was too weak to continue.

If there's one lesson I've learned about mentors, it's that you really should listen when they give advice.

I missed a good deal of the warnings and advice in the beginning of this reversed mentor role due to my high self-opinion of my parenting skills. Regardless of your skills as a parent, take the advice and stories in this book to heart. Heed the words of caution and educate yourself! I have found that raising biological children – for whom I cared from the womb with nourishing food, healthy beverages, and vita-mins -- is *far different* from parenting little ones whose moth-ers had poor nutrition, drank alcohol, and in lieu of vitamins, took drugs.

As Mike and Cheryl began foster parenting, my husband and I watched with amazement. We admired this young couple with their happy brood of biological, foster, and adopted children. Our own children were now growing up and we'd always considered that some day, we too would like to adopt. As we witnessed the ministry in action taking place in the Ellicott home, we were encouraged. We learned from their example that even single income families could adopt through fostercare.

"One day," we said, "we too will add to our already big, happy family!"

We finally believed the time had come -- that the Lord was calling us to fostercare and the possibility of adoption -- in the year 2000. It was a beautiful Sunday afternoon and we were relaxing after church. The kids were here and there throughout the home; my husband and I were in the family room listening to Christian music. When the song *"He,"* by Jars of Clay, came on, the lyrics went straight to our hearts.

The song is about child abuse from a child's perspective. The singer sang in heart-wrenching tones as he unburied the hurting heart of an abused child. On our coffee table, the Sunday newspaper lay open to *Societies Child*. The entire page was covered with pictures of children waiting to find families. Our biological children's happy voices floated through the house as we stared down at these lonely faces.

"Why do you hurt me," the singer cried out through the speakers of our stereo. I looked at my husband; he was trying not to cry, but tears filled his eyes.

"It's time," I said. "God's calling us to rescue children and bring them home." My husband nodded and then we both cried.

Right away, I called my dear friend who was both a foster-mom and an adoptive mom by now. "Cheryl, how do we get set up to do fostercare?" I asked. She explained that my first step was to call a local agency that would take us through the licensing process. We contacted the one she worked with and met with a home study caseworker. Oddly enough, with one thing after another coming up within our family, it took us two full years before we actually became licensed foster parents; normally, it takes just a matter of months. Now I know that God was protecting us. We really had no idea how stressful our home would become after the foster children finally began to arrive.

As we purchased children's furniture, outdoor play equipment, and cute wall borders for the "nursery," which was half of our master bedroom, we were filled with excitement. We were going to provide a happy home for little children who otherwise might have ended up in the Sunday newspaper! Visions of sugarplums danced in our heads as we set up the bassinet beside our own bed.

When our friends, Cheryl and Mike, came over for dinner with their beautiful family -- which had grown to six kids by this time (3 biological, one adopted, and two soon to be adopted), I felt I'd explode with excitement as I watched those beautiful children play. I've always adored children, and as the time to add to our family soon approached, the joy I felt that day as we visited with the Ellicott family is still etched in my mind forever.

I stepped out of the room for some reason or other and Cheryl confided to my husband that she didn't know if I was strong enough to be able to do this. "She'll fall in love with every child and adopt every one that comes up for adoption no matter what..." she told him. "I really don't think she knows what she's getting into!"

They did try to teach me. Both Cheryl and Mike warned us about the serious issues of FAS, FAE, FAES, and others. Was I intimidated by these serious issues? Not at all. I believed that there was no issue or condition our God, our family, and good food, etc., could not *cure*.

When I filled out the questionnaire or "Christmas wish list" as Cheryl puts it, I checked *yes, yes, yes, yes, yes* to so many challenging issues, despite the warnings. I was the older woman; I had it all together. We'd been successful with our biological children and now we were enthusiastic about bringing in some of the babies who were deemed the most difficult.

In hindsight, I was way too plucky; this over-confidence was soon plucked from my heart as I realized I'd landed my entire family in a situation that changed our lives forever. Supermom came crashing down to earth and found out the cape she wore was only an apron after all.

Within a year of our foster/adoption placements, three of our biological kids had moved out. The stress in our home put their dreams for college on hold as they went to work to pay for their apartments. One daughter suffered what seemed to be a nervous breakdown, and for the next few years, she faced extreme difficulties.

Then our youngest biological daughter couldn't take the turmoil anymore. Home life as she'd known it had evaporated and she didn't take the changes well. Formerly an "A" student, she got involved in an unhealthy relationship, dropped out of high school, and ran away from home. Time has passed now and she'd really like to return home and to school, but she has trouble even visiting us for more than a few hours; the stress level in our home is still too much for her.

All three children that we adopted were drug and alcohol exposed prior to birth. Our third and youngest (born less than a year after his sister who'd already been placed with us) came to us after we had been licensed just a year. *Three babies within one year.* Cheryl was right when she warned my husband about what she foresaw as a weakness in me.

No, I could never turn these hurting children away. I love them, and they were my babies from first sight. However, the frequent screaming and howling from a child whose brain has been damaged by alcohol can unravel the nerves of the most patient and loving; these tantrums outlast the tantrums of normal kids and the decibels seem unnaturally high. The tantrums erupt quite suddenly – seemingly without cause; they can last for hours, and on some days, these explosions occur on several occasions. It's difficult for parents, siblings, and even the pets during such times – and we didn't adopt just *one*, but three volatile, needy children.

My hope is in God and His love. We're still strong advocates of good nutrition and believe nurture is powerful medicine, but now I know it'll take an all-out miracle to heal these kids. Adoption is not the end of the story; it is just a beginning.

Each day is a challenge and some days are better than others. On our good days, I take heart; on the bad days, I sometimes wonder if I've made the biggest mistake of my life by taking on such challenges.

Am I a failure? Yes, but God is a winner and He saves failures like me. He gives beauty for ashes... My hope is in Him and Him alone. He uses the foolish things of this world to confound the wise, so I qualify. He can use me!

I think of the missionaries who gave their lives to bring Christ to the lost in foreign lands. Greater love has no man than He who lays down his life for His friends. We are not alone in the mission field... and this is my mission, but it's not at all what I envisioned! I pray that God -- who called us to this new life – will sustain us till the end.

Before adopting, I envisioned the blessings of happy little rescued babies... children laughing, babies smiling and cooing. Reality was something else entirely. Often, it feels like our marriage, our family, and even our sanity is under crushing spiritual attack.

I can relate to the words of Paul the apostle when he says:

> "We do not want you to be uninformed, brothers, about the hardships we suffered... We were under great pressure, far beyond our ability to endure, so that we despaired even of life. Indeed, in our hearts we felt the sentence of death. But this happened that we might not rely on ourselves but on God, who raises the dead."(2 Cor. 1:8-9 NIV)

I expected laughing, smiling, and cooing. Instead, our days and nights are filled with inconsolable screaming, demands that cannot be met, and needs that are overwhelming. These precious little children are very loved; they always have food, hugs, warmth, and a mommy and daddy's love. However, they have intense needs, hurts, and problems that the most loving mommy cannot meet or heal. But Mommy knows someone who can; so I will lead them to Him.

These children, like we who have been adopted into the family of God, have no idea how many thoughts are turned toward them continually. Our adopted children don't see the care and sacrifice that's being shown to them to save them from what could have been a destitute life, but they don't need to know. They just need to know they're loved, cared for, and part of a family. Their older siblings – our biological children -- love them even though four of them were driven from the nest a bit earlier than they'd expected. Our biological children understand that these little adopted ones wouldn't even have had a nest to grow in if not for their willingness to share and our desire to bring them in.

So why was it so hard to share my story with you? Because so often, I feel like a failure. Sometimes I'm still ashamed that I'm not breezing through this. I don't always feel the assurance that everything will someday be okay, but I hope that you can glean from my story that *this truly is war!* As in other wars, without soldiers to stand and fight, there can be no victory. Also, without preparation, soldiers do not stand firmly in battle. Yes, I came into fostercare and adoption wearing rose colored glasses, but I shouldn't have; I was warned. I brushed the warnings away. Now you, the reader, have the opportunity to hear this from an experienced mommy of five and now adoptive mommy to three. Adoption is a real ministry that requires more than you can imagine even with advanced warning. These beautiful children are definitely worth fighting for; they are more than worth the effort! But understand, this is war you're waging! Be prepared and count the cost.

If you have children at home, consider their needs and safety. I had no idea what this would cost my family. I expected we'd remain the happy family we'd always been, and that these little ones would just add more joy. Had I known, I would have waited awhile before I tramped into the battleground with my unsuspecting family. I would have been a whole lot less flippant.

But I had no idea it *was a battleground.*

I want to encourage you to steep this decision in prayer and learn everything you can about FAES and other issues to which you will be exposed. With all that in mind, if the time is right and the calling is there, then gird yourself! Go to war and fight the good fight. There are children waiting to be rescued and waiting for your loving arms.

If you've been given marching orders, then march, but be prepared; put on the full armor of God. You're headed for the front lines and your *very real enemy* doesn't want to let these little souls go.

12

Grandbaby's *First Best* Friend
By Elaine Lambert

"Greater love has no one than this, that he lay down his life for his friends." John 15:13

Our second daughter was an enigma from the start. An amazing little blessing, a gift from heaven that filled me with joy, but also surprise. For starters, I expected a baby boy. Just a hunch, but I was convinced I was carrying a brown-haired, brown-eyed boy; her daddy and I are both brunette and though his eyes are blue - my brown should have dominated. Yet there *she* was; beautiful chubby cheeks, little button nose, sea blue eyes, and sun-kissed copper hair... yes, red. Who'd have ever thought? What a shock. What a gift! So we called her Peaches, with sugar and cream. Yet for all her baby sunshine, there was always the sense of a coming storm.

"She's so serious," said my own mother. "I've never seen a baby worry so much."

What could I say? It was an understatement. Highly intelligent, precocious, overflowing with vibrancy, imagination and potential – yes. But our little girl rarely relaxed and enjoyed life. She was either laughing too loudly or in a state of panic.

From the beginning, she struggled to find a balance. At least, I think that's what was happening. I was struggling too - trying to understand her. When she was learning to talk she panicked if we didn't recognize every word she said. Later, if I told her she'd done something wrong, she'd start scream-ing... *at herself.* As she grew, she was always the loudest, liveliest, most fun person in the room or she was the darkest rain cloud.

Then she hit puberty and entered a new level. She was a three-ring circus with clowns and dancing bears... some-times the whole carnival – balloons, cotton candy, roller coaster... and a haunted house.

Suffice to say, her teen years were turbulent. I've lain awake more nights than I can count praying our daughter is alive. Yet, when she finished high school and went off to college, I was hopeful.

A couple of months later, she'd been kicked out of college and banned from the campus; she was drinking heavily, using drugs, and doing literally everything else we'd raised her to avoid. She came home in tears and saw a little brown puppy in my living room; not just any brown puppy -- a fifteen-hundred-dollar puppy named *Amazing Grace*. I some-times have show dogs and this pup was just passing through on her way to a family.

My daughter loves dogs; I wasn't surprised when her face lit up. She stopped crying and asked, "You got me a puppy?"

Of course I thought, *No way! I love you dearly but this puppy is* most definitely *not for you.* Yet when I prayed, I felt sure that God was saying, *Yes. The puppy is for her.*

It made no sense to me, but I gave her the puppy. She absolutely adored little Gracie. She was touched that I would give her a puppy after she'd bombed on her first try at independence. She and Gracie were inseparable for a time. Again I was hopeful.

Then she began leaving Gracie with me for extended periods while she was out doing *who knows what* and *staying God only knows* where. Eventually she rarely came around and she realized she was neglecting Gracie. She had intense feelings of love for her puppy, yet her lifestyle wasn't suited to nurturing anything. In tears she asked me to find a new family for her sweet, lonely little dog, and I did.

In my prayers, I sometimes asked and wondered if I'd been wrong. *Father, did I mess up? Was I not supposed to give her the puppy?* It seemed like such a mistake. In the end, she had more remorse and heartache because she'd lost something she loved and failed *again.* And yet ... if I heard any reply to my prayers, it was this: *You didn't give her Grace, I did.*

Then I had a dream.

In my dream, I took a pregnant young woman to the doctor; she was someone close to me, but I couldn't see her face. I sat in the room while she had her ultrasound.

Then suddenly, in my dream, I realized I too was expecting a baby. I decided to have an ultrasound as well. As the nurse ran the probe over my stomach, the baby began to move; I could feel it so well. I reached down to see where its hands were; they were on either side of my abdomen. Then the baby stood up as the skin on my stomach cleared like a mist and became translucent as glass. My skin thinned to a film and the baby put its hands in mine and held me tightly. It struggled and lifted its head to gaze up at me. Then my husband was there, and the baby gazed from me to him. The face was tiny, with huge eyes and an ethereal gaze.

I dream a lot, but rarely so vividly. When I do, the dream usually foreshadows coming events. This dream unsettled me; I talked with close friends and we prayed God would prepare my husband and I for whatever was coming.

Nine months later our daughter got pregnant.

She had a steady boyfriend and they were happy about becoming parents. She stopped drinking and doing drugs as soon as she knew she was pregnant. Her boyfriend didn't quit, but he cared enough to leave her home alone while he partied. She accepted this, somewhat, and seemed like an excited, expectant mother. She knitted baby blankets, planned a baby-shower, and kept a baby book. She talked about how much fun they'd have with their child, but I had a deep sense of foreboding...

When the baby was born, his parents took a step toward stability and got married. To celebrate, they got drunk... and stayed that way.

They still talked about the fun things they'd do with their child. They were hopeful, but I really was not. I'd been in their apartment where the shades were always down; there were empty booze bottles in the corners, shadows and piles of trash everywhere... smells and feelings that were far from comforting. It was more like a haunted house than a baby's nursery. No, I was not hopeful. I've seen clowns scare little children, and bears are not safe playmates -- not even dancing bears.

Because baby was born prematurely, he stayed in the hospital for over a month. In the beginning, his mommy was heartbroken that she had to leave him; she returned to the hospital for all of his waking and feeding times. However, things changed when her drinking and drug usage resumed. We didn't realize right away. As grandparents, we visited a couple of times per week at first, so as not to get in the way or threaten the new parents' connection with their child. When we found out his parents weren't consistently showing up, we increased our visits – no longer worrying we'd step on toes. Our concern was now for this precious infant, waiting in the hospital, alone.

Born two months early, with parents who'd taken leave of their senses, he was a delicate little person in an uncertain situation. I nearly cried when I held him. I begged God to protect him and make him big, healthy, and strong – to shower him with love and shield him from the harm and heartache stalking him.

By the time baby was ready to be released from the hospital, his parents' lives and marriage resembled a train-wreck and Child Protective Services were already investigating them, concerned they were unfit. I stood beside my daughter in the hospital, promising CPS and everyone else involved that I would closely monitor the baby and his parents. I didn't need the State to ask this of me, but without my promise, they wouldn't release the baby.

Later, when I was alone with my daughter and grandson, I held him closely, watching as he struggled to lift his head and gaze around the room – it was the same exact face I'd seen in my dream. Premature babies have a bony little face with big owl eyes -- I'd never seen one before, outside my dream. Still holding the baby, I spoke to my daughter, hoping she was listening. "I'll be here to help you. You can ask me anything, anytime. I'm always on your side. Do you know that?"

"Yes, I know," she said, not looking at me, but not exactly looking away.

"From now on," I said, "this baby needs you always on his side -- his best friend. He needs you to take care of him, protect him, and think he's wonderful. When you feel like it, and when you don't. Sometimes you might be his only friend... that's why it's so important." She was looking off into the distance now. "Do you understand?" I asked.

I don't think she heard me. I was talking to myself.

I was talking to myself.

At that moment, I knew I really was talking to myself. I looked down at the perfectly formed infant in my arms; he looked my way and then slowly up toward the ceiling, as if seeing things I couldn't. I believed his mommy would cherish him and they'd have a beautiful relationship... when her mind cleared. But he couldn't wait.

God foresaw this; He knew all along who our grandson's *first* best friend would be and He even shared His secret with me... in a dream.

Our grandson is older now. He's happy, smart, well adjusted – maybe a little spoiled, and certainly a lot cherished. Plus, he's by far the biggest, strongest toddler I've ever known. When God answered my prayer, he *really* answered it.

When the baby was just a few months old, I knew God had prepared me to get a lawyer and take legal custody of him. With his parents lives out of control, it was just a matter of time before CPS would step in again. Would they know or believe the baby had been in my care most of his life and he was safe? I couldn't take that chance; without legal custody I was powerless to protect the baby in my arms.

His parents wanted the best for him, but in their youth and with their serious issues, they were barely managing to keep themselves alive. They saw this and didn't argue when I proposed third party custody.

As time flows on, I hold my breath, watching my daughter's life. I wish I could tell her, "I understand," but she's still an enigma to me. Adrift inside volatile and conflicting emotions, alternately struggling to right her life, then racing headlong toward self-destruction... and I don't know why. The best I can tell her is, "I love you."

I hope she knows I'm still on her side -- always loving her; believing and hoping... fighting her battles with her, though it often looks like I'm against her. Some time ago, her enemy became *herself*. As much as I want to, I won't take her side if it means she, or her beautiful baby will suffer. When she's in her right mind, she wouldn't want me to anyway.

I've seen God heal her from incurable disease, grab hold and remove her from fatal circumstances, and even speak to her in dreams. God gives her grace, again and again and again. She accepts his grace with gladness, then tramples it underfoot.

God has grace abundant and mercies without number. I pray that He'll continue to be patient, keep holding out His mighty hand and offering her His heart. However, He showed me what would happen if my daughter – in her current capacity -- were entrusted with a precious life to nurture. If I stood by and did nothing while she neglected a puppy, I'd feel very badly and would bear the guilt. But *God help me* if I ever have the power to help, yet stand by while my grandchild's cries to go unanswered.

I don't understand, I don't know the rest of the story, but for now I know I must be bold, be strong, and be filled with the power that God offers me. In His strength and His wisdom, I can be a steadfast best friend to my daughter *and* to my grandson. I believe that in their lifetimes, they'll have more best friends... it's been an honor, a privilege and *my divine commission* to be their first.

> "Speak up for those who cannot speak for themselves, for the rights of all who are destitute.
> Speak up and judge fairly; defend the rights of the poor and needy." Proverbs 31:8-9

13

Refuge
By Karen Jessame

How can I explain my daughter Rhia? Wild as our New Zealand hills, like an untamed mountain pony... my sixth child was quite unexpected. It seemed she was born too soon after my fifth. *Another baby so soon after the last one?* I prayed, *"Lord please protect this baby until I get my head around this and accept this as your plan for me."* After a hideously managed labour, Rhia arrived purple and exhausted. This merely hinted at what would come.

She's always been sweet, loving, gifted and intelligent, but also independent and self-assured like none of my other children; she brought drama to my once tidy life. So much drama. She stretched my parenting like none of my others – *stupid, stupid girl*, I have said at times. But which of my other children has caused me to pray so often? Which has, when they're grown, gifted me with a grandchild to help raise – turning my mature years to spring again?

Rhia stopped breathing at six weeks. Afterward, I stayed up night and day with her terrified she would stop breathing again. Alone with her in her battle, feeling emotionally distanced from my husband and other children, I sensed dark oppression around this baby... I was uneasy, unsettled, filled with dread and I thought the devil wanted to take her. *Crazy thought*, I told myself. I was postnatal and overtired. *This is just mental exhaustion...* Yet I prayed again and again, asking God to protect this baby. Eventually both baby and I were admitted to the hospital. After a week or so we came home and carried on as normal.

I remember Rhia at three, with wide eyes and windswept curls about her cheeks, prattling as she trotted along beside me to bring in the milking cow. She *insisted* on carrying a huge bucket. Suddenly the bucket flew into the air, the chatting stopped and Rhia was nowhere to be seen. She had simply disappeared.

There was a hole in the grass alongside the track; I thought she had gone down a pothole in the limestone rocks. My own heart faltered; my sense of losing this child was overwhelming and unexplainable.

Then I heard a wee voice from far below, "Mummy," she said, "I am stuck and I am praying to Jesus cos I am scared!"

I followed the wee voice to where this tiny girl was -- hanging onto a tree root, inside a rock cleft in the fluting of the limestone rock formations, on the bluffs below where we bring in the cow. I climbed down, reached out and pulled her into my arms and to safety. But strangely, this thick dread remained.

I know fear and darkness and I have struggled with something; I struggled with God. With no disrespect to my parents I will tell it how it was: I was beaten as a child; I was kicked, slapped, hit and otherwise abused. I believe my parents loved me and they did the best they knew how... they simply did not know how. Because of my childhood, I've wrestled with God being a father figure. I held back, wanting to be close to Him, but afraid He would reject me. With good reason, for I have done many wrong things. Yet, with Rhia as my daughter, I had no choice – even when I wasn't sure He'd respond to a mere farm wife who had not earned his attention, I cried out to Him anyway.

When Rhia first started school, she decided she did not like it. So she hid herself in the school mail box and arrived home with the mail man.

At nine she went through a plate glass window. I heard the crashing of glass and thought the dog had jumped on the table. But, no, there was Rhia lying on the floor covered in huge shards of glass, with blood on her face, feet, arms and legs. I picked her up and checked for any serious bleeding or glass in her body. We loaded her up traveled an hour and half away to the doctor, with Rhia singing heartily all the way, *Jesus loves me this I know for the Bible tells me so.* Her daddy helped the Doctor sew her up and surprisingly there was little lasting damage.

One time the children had unexplained bruises. Rhia's bruises kept coming for days, so I took her to the Doctor. He questioned me closely: "How are things at home; how is your husband coping; is he well?" Blood tests were taken and I brought my bruised child home.

Two days later the Doctor rang. "Your little girl is very sick you must get her to the hospital immediately."

Again the feeling of absolute dread and boding evil that hounded me with this child. I could not shake it off. Hospital it was and on arrival we met three more children covered in bruises. Relief flooded over me and I was told it was Thrombocyto Paenia Pupura. The first of the affected children went home the next day, the second a day later and finally the third child went home.

But Rhia stayed and stayed and stayed; blood test after blood test... day, after day, after day.

I had five other children at home, three hours away. My husband bundled them all up and came to visit. I missed them so much. I missed my home, my life... yet here I was bound to this child who would not cooperate on any level.

After months of blood tests, bottles of steroids, absolute dread of her hurting herself and bleeding internally, I was done. The rest of the family was suffering, I was strung out and totally over it and the feeling of dread and anxiety was overwhelming. It was too much. I prayed, my Mum prayed, we all prayed -- but blood test after blood test was bad, bad, bad. Finally my husband called the elders of our church and they came with a little bottle of oil -- no fuss, no drama. They poured the oil on Rhia, put their hands on her and prayed.

I cry as I write this... the feeling of dread lifted immediately when they prayed. I saw that Rhia was not only our worry, she was *the Lords*! God would undertake for her... yes she might still be in danger and even obstinate, but the burden was not mine alone. Something evil and nasty and frightful went away that day and has never come back. I cannot explain fully; words cannot express the darkness I felt around this child – some of it was likely guilt, for I had not planned on another baby so soon. I didn't feel joy, excitement or need with this pregnancy. I had to pray for protection of an unborn baby in my own womb for goodness sake. I was so deeply ashamed of those feelings.

Gradually Rhia improved; the steroids were stopped, the blood tests were stopped and we went home to family and farm by the sea. Back home to carry on with everyday tasks, to be a cheerful Mum to the other children, enjoy and encourage my husband, run a house and a business, be a friend to many and have an encouraging word, to rejoice with those whose children do well and not let my sadness overshadow the other aspects of life. All the while feeling like I'm carrying a struggling child in my arms and heart all day long.

When Rhia was a teen, she started smoking pot.

That was bad, but nothing so horrifying as the night my eldest daughter came running down from the shed screaming and crying saying that she thought Rhia was going to die.

My niece, a troubled soul herself was staying with us; she was an influence Rhia didn't need. By the time I got up to the shed these two girls were staggering around incoherently and collapsing. Their eyes were bloodshot and they looked to be blind... they'd been sniffing petrol. Even more shocking was the calf they were sitting with; he could not even get up. I thought they'd never be normal again; *stupid, stupid girls...* Afterward Rhia struggled along with a few brain cells missing and eventually regretted using drugs because it hindered her organisational skills and memory.

Our first five children were outstanding. Apart from the usual kid stuff there were no problems; they were highly respected, successful, lovely, steady and well-liked children. They were awarded prizes of achievement and took responsible roles within the school and polytechs. Both my husband and I also were involved in the school. We were well-respected and well thought of.

You may laugh but within months of Rhia starting at the high school I was labeled *negative, paranoid, aggressive* and two other things I cannot remember. Rhia caused problems, but once she was *labeled a problem*, she was blamed for everything even when she was not involved. Our lovely *model family* was labeled dysfunctional and yes, I resented this. My other children deeply resented Rhia for all the drama, and because the focus seemed always to have been on her. I resented Rhia for bringing such anxiety, shame and difficulty on our whole family, for awhile. But it was also easy to feel I brought it on myself, because I was lazy parenting a sixth child; I thought, *Oh she will be alright; the others are all alright and she will get there...* but Rhia really and truly was different.

At the end of my rope I could not cope any longer and we got the help of an advocate from the child and mental health unit. Rhia was diagnosed with Aspergbergers Syndrome and a programme was put in place at the school. It worked very well, but only until she had no incidence of bad behaviour within a certain time period. Then the support was withdrawn, the teachers went back to treating her like before and at 15 years old Rhia was chucked out of school.

Just before she left school she took on work experience at a racing stable and came home the proud owner of a chucked out horse. That horse became her focus, her love and the path to a more positive life. She threw a saddle on him took him to the beach and galloped into newness. She stayed at home, kicked the drugs, worked in town and saved her money.

Then a few days before her 18th birthday Rhia was in a vehicle accident and her foot was severed except for a small piece of skin and ligament. We gathered at her bedside and prayed; after hours of surgery her toes were pink and she still had a foot.

Months of recovery followed. Her determination was incredible. She stumped around, rode her horse, treasured her pins and screws and plates and x-rays and at last, was hired on to her first job away from home. She was so excited; she tossed her belongings into the car and away she went to a job of breaking horses.

Turned out she was not paid and her boss was little more than a pedophile. After much drama and anxiety our girl came home and started polytech. She did well but something was wrong...

Then one night she rang and told us she was pregnant. She did not tell us *then* that her boss had raped her. She only said she was four months pregnant and was booked to travel to another town to have an abortion. For us at the time it seemed so huge, so dreadful -- the ultimate insult, the stupid girl. We had no idea...

What I did know was I wanted that baby so badly. Already it was part of our family; if the decision was to kill that baby it would never mean it was not there. My feelings were so intense – as if the baby had already been born and I was holding it, having to give it up to be killed... and yet... it was not our decision to make. So I fell back onto my rock in Christ.

"If any man lack wisdom let him ask of God who giveth freely to all men..."

"Oh God in Heaven I need your wisdom," I prayed. "How do I plead for the life of this child and yet give my daughter space? This child will always be ours for years to come. If it's killed now there will be a hole in our family."

I told Rhia if she chose to abort the baby that there would be no going back. If she chose to have this baby – whether to adopt out or keep it -- there would always be an opportunity to save or settle the issue. But once the baby was killed she would have no options. We promised her our unwavering support and that we would help in every way possible. We told her we loved her and that we would love her baby as well.

Over the next few days we waited and worried.

Everyone had their ten cents worth on the situation and their perspective and thoughts. Another overwhelming drama. I began to feel isolated again as when Rhia was a baby and so ill, or when she was at school and using drugs and so needy. I felt again the dread of having done things wrong, of blaming myself.

Was I overcompensating for the bad feelings I'd had over becoming pregnant *again* so soon after a last baby? The last straw was when my husband said abortion might be the best solution. I was furious with him, recalling all my old wounds and every time I'd felt he was not with me in Rhia's battles.

So there I stood one day, hanging out yet another load of washing, with snot and tears running down my face; what a mess. Then suddenly the lights went on in my soul. *Dear God, you care for this child far, far more than I ever could!*

I felt a lightening and laughter welled up within me. The burden lifted away just as it had when the elders prayed over our sick little girl. *Sweet Lord, I give the whole thing to you!* I realized this was the Lord's burden, not mine.

"Dear God, you see the end from the beginning. You are trustworthy. You make no mistakes. Even when you seem silent and we are disappointed with this silence, struggling with it and angry, you are every bit the same God as of our joys and incredible experiences. Nothing about you changes; we can trust you. Please let us honour you with how we handle ourselves through this experience. People will be watching, trying to find an excuse to discount God in their own lives. Do not let us give them reason."

I felt great excitement and anticipation, wanting to see what God could do. I grew, I flew, my soul just lifted and I ended up praising God and feeling a real sense of wonder. I had struggled with seeing God as a *good* Father because if I was naughty as a child there was no going back; wrongs were heaped up, days could go without being spoken to, there was no way to make amends or put things right. I did some real, real bad things at times and lived with a sense of fear and dread. I put this on God too, feeling very uncomfortable asking for things – I thought I had to earn the right to ask.

But at last I saw something: the eternal God is our refuge and underneath are the everlasting arms.

God is in His heaven above us. God reaches down to men in grace and love and mercy. Who needs refuge? A refuge is a hiding place, a place of healing and provision. Everything is there for us in God; we hurt, we cry, we do things wrong, we are attacked, we are challenged, we are scared. If we fall His everlasting arms are underneath us -- not on top to shield up from every trouble, not raised up to strike us for doing wrong things, not behind his back to ignore us because we are naughty or disobedient, but underneath us to catch us.

I'm no longer afraid to feel a sense of excitement even in the darkest hour, because He is a *good* Father. Yes, Satan means this or that for evil, but God can and will use it for good.

Not long after that Rhia told us she'd decided to keep her baby. In due time she gave birth to a beautiful baby girl.

Our granddaughter is four years old now. She has lived with us and with her Mummy. Things have been tough -- real tough. There have been tears, laughter, joy, sorrow... and some dread. I still feel all these things from time to time. But our grand baby is such a lovely little girl; she has fitted into the family like the precious gift she is. She is dearly loved by all her aunties and uncles and has a very special bond with her granddaddy. She brings us much joy and delight.

When my daughter stumbles, I recall God's arms are holding me, catching me when I would fall. I remember Rhia's wee voice from far below saying, "Mummy, I am stuck and I am praying to Jesus cos I am scared!" I remember when I was that wee child, but I did not cry out – afraid that only beatings would come. My parents would not beg God to protect me, but might likely hurt me.

Maybe the sense of dread I experienced was tied to guilt; maybe it was about what *might have been*, without Jesus; but *He is here* and we are crying out to Him... because we are scared. So, even today, I will climb down, reach out and pull Rhia into my arms and to safety – for as long as she needs me to.

EPILOGUE

I received a letter the other day sealed tightly in a cute little envelope with the words *"Mommy Only!"* in bright purple on the front.

Sometimes I'm afraid to open these letters. I began getting them a couple years ago -- slid under my bedroom door, hidden under my pillow, or discreetly tucked into my pocket as we passed in the hall.

The author of these letters was always the same; my adopted daughter. The same dear girl who for years nearly drove me insane with her bizarre and horrible behaviors and who on so many occasions I honestly wished I'd never met... but only for the first nine or ten years after she came into our family.

But then... when she was a young teen, something happened.

Suddenly she began writing me these letters, tucking them into small envelopes and delivering them when no one was watching. At first, they were the kind of letters that left me speechless; they needed to be burned after reading. She'd had an encounter with God and realized she needed to confess -- to Mom -- *all* of the times she'd lied, stolen, cheated, and otherwise... broken the rules; this process took many months and *many long letters.*

When there was nothing left to confess, the letters stopped for awhile. Words can't describe what it's like to watch a total heart-change, which is *the answer to your prayers*, while also learning that someone's behavior was much worse than you'd ever imagined.

Joy... anger... gratitude... bitterness... amazement? In the end, I chose to let the gratitude and amazement reign, even though it wasn't easy. As a child, I was not the easiest girl to parent, and I've had that same life-changing encounter with God; I need to remind myself of this often.

There were no "*Mommy Only!*" letters for awhile. During that time, I watched her; sometimes wondering if the change would last. I chided myself for wondering -- but I've worked with kids (more specifically troubled kids), for a long, long time; I've seen countless "conversions without fruit" and only a few that produce real change.

Thankfully, with my adopted daughter, it didn't take long before I had to admit it was real.

One day, the letters started again; this time they were different. No burning required! Each time I received one, it's as if someone were reading my mind and knew exactly what I needed to hear to encourage me to go on. Often, I opened the card and there was just a scripture -- or many scriptures -- written in bright colors, with swirls and little flowers emphasizing the important points.

This latest card was no exception. It arrived when I was deeply troubled, to put it mildly, over the current behavior of our younger adopted daughter. Since my name is on this book as author, I won't mention all of the troubling behaviors we deal with constantly. I'll let you use your imagination.

Sometimes I just want to look at our younger adopted daughter and say, "GET BETTER ALREADY! Act like a normal girl! *Stop being neurotic!*" Actually, I think I *have* said that. Sorry, but I have my moments, too. Anyway, it didn't work. Her response was, "Okay. Please tell me how to stop, and I will." Not one of my brighter moments.

So my latest "*Mommy Only!*" card came on a day when I felt like giving up. Times like this, God knows I need a friend; somebody who really understands that *adoption can be very difficult* and encourages me to never grow weary in doing good.

Mommy Only!

Dearest Mommy,

I just want to tell you how thankful I am for all you have done for me.

Thank you for praying for me and for the way you correct me. I am glad God has chosen you to be my Mom. You have done a great job and He has given you wisdom to do it. I know I was a very difficult girl to take care of, and you probably even don't know how troubled and sad inside I was; more than you know.

I want to tell you, or remind you that I was just like my sister, even worse! I've been watching you and you're doing an awesome job. I just hope she "will come to" her "senses and escape from the trap of the devil who has taken" her "captive to do his will."

God has done it for me, he can do it for her!

"Those who oppose him he must gently instruct in the hope that God will grant them repentance, leading them to the knowledge of the truth, and that they will come to their senses and escape from the trap of the devil, who has taken them captive to do his will." 2 Timothy 2:25-26

Good job! Excellent!

Friends, *thank you* from the bottom of my heart for reading through this entire book. I pray it's given you insight into some of the difficulties that you may face as foster or adoptive parents. We haven't talked about the many blessings and joys of adoption. There are plenty of books about those and I encourage you to read and believe them.

The world of adoption is filled with beauty... *but I think you already knew that.*

If you're being called, God will give you the strength to do His will; so get ready now. Put aside your fears and follow Jesus wherever He leads you.

I'll see you on the other side and you can tell me all about the children you've loved and the miracles you've seen.

GLOSSARY

Americans have changed a lot in the past fifty years in regard to adoption. In the 1960s and 70s private infant adoptions were at their highest number ever, as society's views on *sex outside of marriage* loosened and the baby boomer generation reached child-bearing years. The number of child adoptions by unrelated adoptive parents reached its peak in 1970, with 89,200, but then began to decline as society relaxed its views of single parenting, abortion and birth control. The number of infants being placed for adoption in the U.S. drastically dwindled after that, and parents hoping to adopt began considering international adoption and adoptions of children from the fostercare system.

The following glossary touches on the basics that you need to get started. Please keep in mind that the trends and rules surrounding adoption vary from state to state and change often. This information was correct at the time of writing, but may have changed. For a more comprehensive glossary, please visit a website such as www.adoption.com.

COMMON TYPES OF ADOPTION:

Domestic Adoption/Private Adoption: In 2008, the cost for domestic adoption through an agency or adoption lawyer (after all fees are tallied) is estimated to be between $20,000.00 and $65,000.00.

International Adoption: In 2009, the cost to adopt internationally (after all fees are tallied) is estimated to be between $40,000.00 and $65,000.00.

Adoption through Fostercare:

These are the main THREE WAYS to adopt through the USA Fostercare System:

1. *Foster Child Adoption:* An estimated 70% of all children adopted through the fostercare system are adopted either by relatives or their foster parents. Parents hoping to adopt infants through the fostercare system will almost always succeed if they become part of the fostercare system and care for infants in that capacity for some time. In many states, foster parents are given first choice to adopt if the child becomes available for adoption, but they will most likely see others returned to biological families and must be able to say goodbye. As of the year 2010, the fees for adopting foster children are still often waived and families often receive a monthly subsidy (throughout the childhood years) to help offset the costs of raising the children. (See *Adoption Subsidy* for more information.)

2. *Fost-Adopt Program:* Licensed Fost-Adopt parents take in *only* children who are identified as extremely likely to become legally available, (though *not yet* legally available); these might be infants, toddlers, or even older children. Sometimes called "Legal Risk," this program runs two "plans" simultaneously: a plan toward adoption and one toward biological family reunification. Running dual plans is an attempt to have the child permanently settled *somewhere* sooner. The Fost-Adopt parents intend to adopt if the biolog-

ical parents' rights are severed, but the Fost-Adopt parent is required to support both plans.

3. *Waiting-Child Adoption:* Parents become licensed to adopt through a local agency, then they wait for a "match" to be made between themselves and a child or sibling group who are already legally free and waiting for adoption. The waiting children are almost always special needs (as described below). During this waiting period, they may rely upon their licensing worker to search, but they may also browse photo books or photo listings of available children and contact the child's case manager to be considered.

OTHER FORMS OF ADOPTION or CUSTODY:

Relative Adoption/Grandparent Adoption: Many grandparents, aunts and uncles are raising their grandchildren, nieces or nephews these days. In addition to adoption, there are many other legal options for caregivers, and each state's laws vary. Websites such as www.adoption.com and www.adopting.org have reference libraries to help you research your options. You must follow legal procedures if you want the child and your guardianship status protected.
Do not simply write up an agreement between yourself and the biological parents, notarize it and then assume it protects you and the child. It most likely will not. *Expect to hire a lawyer.*

NOTE: Many states offer "subsidized guardianship" for relatives who are raising and have legal custody of children that were previously in the state's custody. The subsidy consists of monthly support payments, from the state to the family.

☀THER TERMS:

SPECIAL NEEDS: *Disabilities, minority race, age, sibling status, and at-risk* are categories considered *"Special Needs."* A child adopted through fostercare and classified as *special needs* may qualify for adoption assistance payments (subsidies). The monthly amount depends upon the type and severity of the need. The current economy also dictates what assistance payments are available.

DISABILITIES include mental, physical, or emotional disabilities and disorders, which can range from mild to severe. Behavioral problems fall under the *emotional disabilities* classification.

MINORITY RACE is often considered to be a *special need*, especially if the child is male because the majority of adoptive families are seeking non-minority race, infant *girls*.

AGE may be considered a *special need*; each state differs, and ages may be classified differently depending upon race. Typically, a child over age 5-8 years might be considered *special needs* aged.

SIBLING GROUPS (three or more) are often harder to place, and therefore sometimes classified as *special needs*. This is especially true if other factors are present, like disabilities and minority race. However, small sibling groups (two members) of healthy children usually are not classified as *special needs*; they are not hard to find homes for.

"AT-RISK" CHILDREN are babies exposed to alcohol, drugs, abuse, neglect, and those with genetic pre-dispositions to mental illness and physical disabilities; they may be currently healthy.

ADOPTION SUBSIDY: *"Subsidy and Purchase of Service"* means the state is offering to provide monthly "reimbursement" payments to qualifying parents who adopt *special needs* children. This saves the state money (paying to keep the child in shelter or foster homes is more expensive) and it allows parents to adopt who would not have been able to otherwise due to financial constraints. A monthly reimbursement might be between $300 and $1000 per child, or more if the *special needs* are considered severe; this subsidy continues, usually, until the child turns 18, or sometimes till 21 if they're consistently attending school and cannot graduate or pass the GED.

HOME STUDY: (Also called *"adoption study"):* This written report contains the findings of the social worker who meets with the prospective adoptive parents. The social worker visits their home and investigates the health, medical, criminal, family, and home background of the prospective adoptive parents (and of any other individuals living in the home). Whichever agency does the home study will depend upon the type of adoption you pursue. The home study helps the court determine whether the adoptive parents are qualified to adopt a child, based on criteria established by state law.

PARENT PROFILE: Couples create a "Parent Profile" by which a birthmother may find and choose them to adopt her baby. Included in the profile is usually a *"Dear Birthmother Letter"* addressed to the potential birth mother; it may explain the adoptive parents' reasons for wanting to adopt, their parenting philosophy, details about their marriage, and their religious or spiritual beliefs. If you're listed publicly as a *parent hoping to adopt*, beware of scams. Scam artists may find you via a Parent Profile book, website, or even on an adoption forum/email list. Scammers contact parents, claiming they have a baby to be adopted, and then ask for money. Money changes hands in legitimate adoptions, too, so it's *not easy to spot a scam*. The stories may be quite complicated and convincing.

When contacted by birthparents or others claiming to have a child for you, respond carefully (in case it's legitimate) and let them know you have a good lawyer (and that you've shared their correspondence with him), who is helping you understand the process. This should *not* scare away a legitimate contact, but will usually deter scam artists. Check this website for more safety information: www.adoptionscams.net

OPEN ADOPTION: Every adoption of this type will be different, based on the type of relationship to which the birthparents and the adoptive parents agree. In some open adoptions, the birthparent and the adoptive family simply have ongoing communication about the child. In other cases, the child also has an ongoing relationship with the birthparent.

CLOSED ADOPTION/TRADITIONAL ADOPTION: In these adoptions, the birth family and the adoptive family do not communicate or share any identifying information. The adoptive parents may receive non-identifying health and other background information on the child or birth family before adoption. The birthparents may also receive non-identifying information about the adoptive parents. The adoption files will be sealed after the adoption.

LIFE BOOK: A personal album chronicling a child's history. Life books vary depending upon who creates them. Some include information about past history, birthparents, biological relatives, and cultural heritage.

Life books are put together by social workers, foster or adoptive parents, birthparents or other relatives – often because they want the child to feel like they have roots and known history.

Adoption Disruption or Dissolution:

DISRUPTION: Usually refers to an adoption that's canceled before finalization, even though the adoptive parents were identified as the parents to adopt and the child might have been placed in their home for a period of time. The term may sometimes refer to any failed adoption attempt.

DISSOLUTION: A reversal or voiding of an adoption *after* it's legal finalization. This may occur for a variety of reasons, but most commonly:

1. It was a poor match; the parents weren't prepared, qualified or aware of the needs and challenges of the child.

2. The circumstances of the child or the adoptive family have changed substantially since the adoption; a continuation of the relationship is impractical or impossible.

NOTE: Sometimes a family attempts to dissolve an adoption but the judge denies the request, removes the child, and orders the adoptive parents to pay child support to the state until the child turns 18.

UNDERSTANDING WHAT'S *NOT BEING SAID:*

In the world of adoption, people often use terms that imply truth, but make negative facts *more palatable*. Their motives may be to help and protect the child, but if you as a potential adoptive parent don't understand *what's not being said*, you'll be blind sided with things you're not prepared to deal with. Here's just one example:

LACK OF BOUNDARIES: Read the following description of a 7-year-old girl. I've italicized some key words or phrases.

> "She is in therapy to help her deal with past trauma, to *develop appropriate* peer and adult *interactions*, and strengthen her *very soft personal boundaries*. Her treatment and safety plan mandate that she have *line-of-sight supervision* at home, school, and in the community because of her *poor boundaries*... She was placed in a therapeutic foster home with a mother-and-*father* family. The placement came to a close quickly, because her behavior escalated out of control. She now resides in a foster home with a *mom only*... Because of her issues, she will do best in a female household, and *must be the only child* or the youngest of much older sisters who will be emotionally and socially healthy role models for her. There should be *no family pets*."

That doesn't sound too bad, does it? However, what they're implying (but not saying) is that this child acts out sexually toward any men with whom she comes into contact with. She's okay around women, but she victimizes smaller children and animals. She must never be let "out of sight." Children with these issues often try to develop a *special* relationship with one parent to *take them away* from their spouse; however, "boundaries" does not always imply abnormal sexual behaviors. Whenever you hear this word, *ask what the boundary issues are!*

The previous is just one example. Be aware that the world of adoption is just like the rest of life – people are not entirely forthcoming. When they *are required* to share the facts, they'll often dress them up to fit the occasion.

As with all of your life, approach every adoption decision with *lots of prayer* and a *heart willing to yield* and let God lead.

BIBLE BASICS

For those who want to read the Bible but get overwhelmed or don't understand it, this simple Bible Study highlights the main points of the Bible. Children and adults alike may use this to jumpstart their Bible reading. Pray for understanding before you begin and you'll find it even easier. Be sure to look up the scriptures listed.

God loves you.

He loves you more than anyone ever has or ever will. He made you to be his friend. He thinks about you more than you think about yourself. He wants you to know him, like he knows you.

He has a beautiful and important plan for your life.

"God so loved the world that He gave His one and only Son, that whoever believes in Him shall not perish, but have eternal life." (John 3:16 NIV)

"How precious concerning me are your thoughts, O God! How vast is the sum of them! Were I to count them, they would outnumber the grains of sand..." (Psalms 139:17-18 NIV)

[Christ speaking] "I came that they might have life, and might have it abundantly" [that it might be full and meaningful]. (John 10:10 NIV)

Most people aren't living a meaningful life as God's friends. We have a big problem; God is all things right and righteous. He is love and truth; He is holy and perfect -- we're not.

We've done wrong things (sin); it came natural to us...

Our sin separated us from God; now we can't hear him when he calls and our guilt makes him turn his face away when we pray.

> "All have sinned and fall short of the glory of God." (Romans 3:23 NIV)

> "The wages of sin is death" [spiritual separation from God]. (Romans 6:23 NIV)

> "... the eyes of the Lord are on the righteous and his ears are attentive to their prayer, but the face of the Lord is against those who do evil." (1 Peter 3:12 NIV)

We might try to convince ourselves that we're okay. We may compare ourselves with others and say, "See? I'm not that bad." The world is filled with false religions, psychology, and philosophies that tell us we're good enough; we may believe and try each one, but they won't set us free.

No, not even religion can save us – we've already broken one law thus we might as well have broken them all; we can't be good enough to make up for it.

Even if we're good compared with most people, there's still a canyon of guilt between our perfect God and us.

Our souls remain hopeless; our spirits lifeless and lonely.

"For whoever keeps the whole law and yet stumbles at just one point is guilty of breaking all of it." (James 2:10 NIV)

"My guilt has overwhelmed me like a burden too heavy to bear. My wounds fester and are loathsome because of my sinful folly. I am bowed down and brought very low; all day long I go about mourning." (Psalm 38:4-6 NIV)

However, God loves you and he made a bridge over this canyon.

"... the law requires that nearly everything be cleansed with blood, and without the shedding of blood there is no forgiveness." (Hebrews 9:22 NIV)

God sent a savior to suffer and pay the penalty for our sin.

Jesus Christ was the only person who ever lived a perfect and sinless life.

He claimed to be God in human form; He proved it by fulfilling hundreds of prophecies, healing sick people, casting demons out of others, bringing dead people back to life, and by rising from the dead himself.

His death was an acceptable substitute for ours, because unlike everyone else, he was not dying for his own sins; He was dying for ours.

There are many false beliefs and useless religions, but (this is important!) there's only ONE bridge to God!

Jesus Christ is God's ONLY provision for forgiveness from sin; through Him, we can know God's love and plan for our lives.

He Died in Our Place

"God demonstrates His own love toward us, in that while we were yet sinners, Christ died for us." (Romans 5:8 NIV)

He Rose From the Dead

"Christ died for our sins... He was buried... He was raised on the third day, according to the Scriptures... He appeared to Peter, then to the twelve. After that He appeared to more than five hundred..." (1 Corinthians 15:3-6 NIV)

He Is the Only Way to God

"Jesus said to him, 'I am the way, and the truth, and the life; no one comes to the Father, but through Me.'" (John 14:6 NIV)

"' Where, O death, is your victory? Where, O death, is your sting?' The sting of death is sin, and the power of sin is the law. But thanks be to God! He gives us the victory through our Lord Jesus Christ." (1 Corinthians 15:55-57 NIV)

If we don't know Jesus, we are not God's friends yet because we're still stained by the things we've done wrong; we're separated from God who is perfect; we can't be good enough.

However, we can cross over on the bridge God worked so hard to give us.

"Therefore, my brothers, I want you to know that through Jesus the forgiveness of sins is proclaimed to you. Through him everyone who believes is justified from everything you could not be justified from by the law of Moses." (Acts 13: 38-39 NIV)

"... a man is not justified by observing the law, but by faith in Jesus Christ. So we, too, have put our faith in Christ Jesus that we may be justified by faith in Christ and not by observing the law, because by observing the law no one will be justified." (Galatians 2:16 NIV)

We can be God's friend. We can be set free from our sin, guilt, and shame. We can accept Jesus' payment for our sin. We can be forgiven and considered righteous, because Jesus wants to share *His* righteousness with us. What does he ask for in exchange?

Us! He wants us wholly; hearts, minds, bodies and souls.

"Love the Lord your God with all your heart and with all your soul and with all your mind and with all your strength." (Mark 12:30 NIV)

We must believe. We must ask Jesus to take away our guilt, give us clean hearts, and carry us over the bridge and into friendship with God.

[Jesus said] "I tell you the truth, whoever hears my word and believes him who sent me has eternal life and will not be condemned; he has crossed over from death to life." (John 5:24 NIV)

"He commanded us to preach to the people and to testify that he [Jesus] is the one whom God appointed as judge of the living and the dead. All the prophets testify about him that everyone who believes in him receives forgiveness of sins through his name." (Acts 10: 42-43 NIV)

"If we claim to be without sin, we deceive ourselves and the truth is not in us. If we confess our sins, he is faithful and just and will forgive us our sins and purify us from all unrighteousness." (1 John 1:8,9 NIV)

If we believe, are forgiven, and ask, God will send His Holy Spirit to live in our hearts. The spirit will explain spiritual things to us, give us power to change, and help us discover the important plans God has for our lives.

> "At one time we too were foolish, disobedient, deceived and enslaved by all kinds of passions and pleasures. We lived in malice and envy, being hated and hating one another. But when the kindness and love of God our Savior appeared, he saved us, not because of righteous things we had done, but because of his mercy. He saved us through the washing of rebirth and renewal by the Holy Spirit, whom he poured out on us generously through Jesus Christ our Savior, so that, having been justified by his grace, we might become heirs having the hope of eternal life." (Titus 3:7 NIV)

> "I will pray to the Father, and He will give you another Helper, [the Holy Spirit] that He may abide with you forever." (John 14:16 NIV)

If you believe the things you've read in this Bible study, talk to God about them. Ask him to forgive your sin through the work Jesus did. Ask him to fill you with his Holy Spirit and open your eyes so you can understand him.

Begin to read the Bible and pray that he will explain it to you.

Breinigsville, PA USA
26 January 2011
254176BV00001B/2/P

9 780984 359943